THE GREAT PHYSICIAN'S

R^x *for*

CHRONIC FATIGUE AND FIBROMYALGIA

JORDAN RUBIN

with Joseph Brasco, M.D.

THOMAS NELSON
Since 1798

NASHVILLE DALLAS MEXICO CITY RIO DE JANEIRO BEIJING

Copyright © 2007 by Jordan Rubin

All rights reserved. No portion of this book may be reproduced, stored in a retrieval system, or transmitted in any form or by any means—electronic, mechanical, photocopy, recording, scanning, or other—except for brief quotations in critical reviews or articles, without the prior written permission of the publisher.

Published in Nashville, Tennessee. Thomas Nelson is a trademark of Thomas Nelson, Inc.

Thomas Nelson Inc. titles may be purchased in bulk for educational, business, fundraising, or sales promotional use. For information, please e-mail SpecialMarkets@ThomasNelson.com.

Scripture quotations noted NKJV are from the NEW KING JAMES VERSION®. Copyright © 1979, 1980, 1982 by Thomas Nelson, Inc. Used by permission. All rights reserved.

Scripture quotations noted KJV are from the KING JAMES VERSION.

Scripture quotations noted NIV are from the HOLY BIBLE: NEW INTERNATIONAL VERSION®. Copyright © 1973, 1978, 1984 by International Bible Society. Used by permission of Zondervan Publishing House. All rights reserved.

Library of Congress Cataloging-in-Publication Data

Rubin, Jordan.
    The great physician's RX for chronic fatigue and fibromyalgia / by Jordan Rubin, with Joseph Brasco.
        p. cm.
    Includes bibliographical references and index.
    ISBN 978-0-7852-1913-2
    1. Chronic fatigue syndrome—Alternative treatment. 2. Fibromyalgia—Alternative treatment. 3. Chronic fatigue syndrome—Religious aspects—Christianity. 4. Fibromyalgia—Religious aspects—Christianity. I. Brasco, Joseph. II. Title.
    RB150.F37R83 2007
    616'.0478—dc22   2007014384

Printed in the United States of America

07 08 09 10 11 QW 5 4 3 2

CONTENTS

INTRODUCTION

Down for the Count

Caryn Edens was born in Stockton, California, in the mid-1950s, the oldest of four children. Dad was a circulation manager for the *Modesto Bee* newspaper; Mom was a real estate agent.

Caryn came of age in the late 1960s, a turbulent time of unrest and rebellion, of antiwar demonstrations and hippie love-ins. "Peace and Free Love" was the anthem of the day. Like her peers, Caryn wore tattered blue jeans, peasant blouses, rainbow beads, and other groovy clothing such as tie-dye shirts and patchwork pants.

I'm told by my parents that there was another cultural event happening at that time—the so-called "Jesus Movement" that arose on the West Coast in the late sixties and early seventies. The Holy Spirit swept through the hippie counterculture, bringing tens of thousands of those disenchanted with the status quo into God's family. Their lively worship services are said to have paved the way for the development of contemporary Christian music, or CCM.

One of those persons swept up by the outpouring of the Holy Spirit was Caryn Edens. "I was a Jesus freak," she said, "and we were downright unpopular. I was never a doper. I hung out with other Christians at school. I ate lunch with other Jesus freaks and attended a before-school Bible study in one of the teacher's classrooms. I carried two Bibles around Downey High, a King James Version and a Living Bible. Looking back, they were awesome chastity belts."

After graduating, Caryn married her high school sweetheart—a policeman—and had two children, a boy and a girl. The marriage, however, could not survive the strain of a son with severe attention deficit disorder issues or the tension of living with a husband working in a high-profile, life-or-death profession. After thirteen years, the marriage was over.

And Caryn's health problems were just beginning.

Raising a high-maintenance son with ADD and dealing with the difficulty of being a single-parent mom piled loads of stress on Caryn's shoulders. In 1993, she was supporting the family by working for a cemetery, selling plots and headstones. She noticed that when she got up in the morning, she experienced dizziness or a sensation of whirling. Those feelings of seasickness continued throughout the day and were often accompanied by nausea and occasional vomiting. All she had to do was stand up and her world would start spinning. She saw several doctors who agreed that she had a classic case of vertigo, the "spinning" disorder thought to be caused by an inner ear imbalance.

Since that diagnosis nearly fifteen years ago, Caryn has had her hands full with a long list of ailments, including high blood pressure, numbness in the feet, back pains, bowel problems, and migraine headaches. Her health wasn't helped when her two prodigal children added a few bricks to the stressful load she was carrying on her shoulders. Her daughter stole her car at age thirteen, ran away, and came home pregnant at fourteen. Her son got shot in the back of the head with a pellet gun, overdosed on drugs, and survived a stabbing by a troubled Vietnam vet.

Several years ago, Caryn developed a tumor on her adrenal

gland, which was removed, and her gallbladder failed. The surface of her eyes mysteriously dried up, so she had to constantly add eye drops to keep them lubricated. Her neck and spine developed scoliosis. But most of all, Caryn couldn't remember the last time she woke up feeling refreshed and full of energy. Instead, when she tried to get out of bed, every muscle in her body shouted out in pain. Caryn wondered who had unplugged her power supply.

She was in and out of doctors' offices, seeking clues for why a variety of illnesses lay claim to her body. Then in 2001, one of her physicians believed he had the answer. "I think you have fibromyalgia," he said, which is a widespread musculoskeletal disorder in the muscles, ligaments, and tendons and is closely associated with chronic fatigue syndrome. A second doctor confirmed the diagnosis.

When she was told that modern medicine didn't have much to offer in terms of treatment, Caryn gamely persevered in the midst of her health trials. Her second husband, John, was supportive and loving, but he was an ex-alcoholic prone to binge eating. Once he brought home ten pounds of candy and three bags of chips for them to snack on. "I know that when John would bring the junk food home, that pulled me down," she said.

Then Caryn heard that I was coming to her church, Calvary Temple Worship Center, to speak about the Great Physician's prescription for health and wellness. I'll let her pick up the story here:

Before Jordan came to Modesto, I knew I was fighting for my life. I didn't want to continue living as I had been doing since 1993. I wanted to get well. I wanted to *live*.

I had been hanging on to Deuteronomy 30:19: "I call heaven and earth as witnesses today against you, that I have set before you life and death, blessing and cursing; therefore choose life, that both you and your descendants may live" (NKJV).

I was excited to hear that Jordan was coming to speak at our church because I had heard good things about him and what he had to say. When Jordan urged us to eat foods that God created—not junk foods with man-made ingredients—I hung on his every word. I sat in the audience and thought about how much I wanted to choose life. I thought about how my regular stops at Taco Bell, Burger King, and Jack in the Box could have been contributing to many of my symptoms. My food choices, I had to admit, weren't that good.

After Jordan spoke that Sunday morning, Calvary Temple hosted a church-wide health program called the "7 Weeks of Wellness," and more than 360 men and women participated. Kelli Williams, the health ministries pastor at Calvary Temple and a registered nurse, facilitated the classes using video teaching by Jordan. I stopped the fast food runs and eating anything fried. I shopped at Trader Joe's, which sells a lot of organic and whole foods, for omega-3 eggs, old-fashioned oatmeal, and fresh berries. I began sautéing with coconut oil and only adding olive oil to dressings and recipes. I made it a point to eat as many raw fruits and vegetables as I could. I snacked on almonds, pumpkin seeds, and raisins instead of salty potato chips. I kept a supply of dried plums in my purse so that I would have something to eat if I got hungry doing errands. Since I started the Great Physician's prescription, I've lost approximately twenty-five pounds, and I see myself losing more weight.

I believe the Bible's health plan is healing me of my fibromyalgia pain and other symptoms, and for me, relief is a real joy.

I wish Caryn all the best, especially after years of dealing with constant fatigue and unrelenting pain. Chronic fatigue syndrome (CFS) and fibromyalgia (FM) are no fun, and I speak from experience because I suffered from symptoms of both afflictions when I faced significant health challenges shortly after my freshman year of college. As I chronicled in my book *The Great Physician's Rx for Health and Wellness,* I began experiencing nausea, stomach cramps, and horrible digestive problems out of the blue back in 1994. The constant diarrhea was the worst. That summer I was a counselor at a Christian youth camp, and I'd be out on the ropes course with the kids when suddenly I'd have this gigantic urge to go. After excusing myself to the other counselors, I'd walk *very quickly*—running was out of the question—to the nearest toilet, which was one of those hole-in-the-floor jobs. It was humiliating!

That was the start of a two-year health odyssey. I was seen by seventy doctors and health experts, ranging from traditional to alternative, who treated me for symptoms of irritable bowel syndrome, Crohn's disease, diabetes, arthritis, and anemia, as well as symptoms of chronic fatigue syndrome and fibromyalgia. Believe me: I'm a fellow pilgrim down the road you're traveling.

Chronic fatigue syndrome and fibromyalgia present themselves through persistent, overwhelming symptoms of fatigue and feelings of exhaustion. Thankfully, CFS and FM have become better understood in the last decade or so. Today they're viewed as a complex and continual cycle of symptoms that dramatically lower the quality of one's life.

As victims such as Caryn Edens understand, chronic fatigue syndrome and fibromyalgia are horribly debilitating afflictions that share many of the same symptoms:

- persistent headaches
- bouts of insomnia
- irritating muscle and joint pain
- memory and concentration lapses
- fevers
- environmental sensitivities
- loss of appetite
- food allergies
- mood swings
- muscle spasms
- nasal congestion
- candidiasis
- sensitivity to light and heat

- night sweats
- swollen lymph nodes

The main difference between the two conditions is that chronic fatigue syndrome's primary symptom is extreme fatigue, while the most prevalent symptom of fibromyalgia is widespread muscle aches and pain.

The Centers for Disease Control (CDC) says that approximately four million Americans have CFS, or 1.3 percent of the U.S. population.[1] A similar number of Americans (3.7 million) have fibromyalgia, according to the National Institute of Arthritis and Musculoskeletal and Skin Diseases (NIAMS) at the National Institutes of Health (NIH).[2] This debilitating malady has affected such celebrities as the Duchess of Kent, soccer star Michelle Akers, and jazz pianist Keith Jarrett.[3]

Two new studies from the *Archives of General Psychiatry* suggest that traumatic events in childhood, as well as periods of emotional instability, can be associated with the development of chronic fatigue syndrome.[4] Chronic fatigue syndrome and fibromyalgia are much more common in females than in males, and symptoms usually present themselves in young adulthood, starting gradually and slowly increasing in intensity. This disparity could be because women are more willing to talk to their doctors about things such as tiredness and pain. But from an anecdotal perspective, I can tell you that when I'm out speaking and meeting people, I encounter nine times more women than men with CFS and FM. To make matters worse, when women with fibromyalgia are menstruating, they seem to have horrific side effects during that time of the month.

CONVENTIONAL TREATMENT

CFS and FM are among the most mysterious and controversial maladies of the last twenty years. Back in the 1980s, chronic fatigue syndrome was waved off as "yuppie flu" by medical practitioners because the condition seemed to be concentrated among young, urban, white professionals. Some male doctors dismissed it as a "head case" disease, since predominantly women came to their offices complaining about feeling tired all the time. Others call it "a disease with a thousand names."

Doctors find is difficult to diagnose chronic fatigue syndrome or fibromyalgia because there are no lab tests for them. If you enter a doctor's office complaining about feeling tired all the time, he or she will ask about your physical and mental health, perform a physical exam, and order urine and blood tests to see if something else could be causing your symptoms.

Doctors will not officially diagnose you with these conditions until your tests come back negative for other conditions or diseases and you have been extremely tired or in great pain for six months or more. They also want you to answer yes to at least four of the following questions:

- Do you forget things or have a hard time focusing?
- Do you feel tired—even after sleeping?
- Do you have muscle pain or aches?
- Do you feel discomfort or "out of sorts" for more than twenty-four hours after doing something active?

- Do you have headaches of a new type or strength?
- Do you have tender lymph nodes in the neck or under the arm?
- Do you have a sore throat or a constant cough?
- Do you have feelings of depression?

Once a diagnosis has been established for CFS and FM, physicians don't have a whole lot they can offer. They often suggest lifestyle changes—admonishing patients to stop doing so much during the day or eliminating activities that are exhausting. Some encourage mild forms of exercise but remind their patients that too much exertion can only make them even more tired. Others recommend taking over-the-counter pain relievers such as Advil, Motrin, or Aleve, or they offer to write a prescription for antidepressants to improve sleep. No medications have been specifically approved for the treatment of chronic fatigue syndrome or fibromyalgia, however.

The Divided Mind
by Dr. Joseph Brasco

I recently read a book by John Sarno, M.D., an eighty-three-year-old physician who is a professor of clinical rehabilitation medicine at New York University Medical Center and is still treating patients.

The Divided Mind: The Epidemic of Mindbody Disorders explores the crucial interaction between a rational, conscious mind and the repressed feelings of emotional pain that are the basis for many "mindbody" disorders, as he calls them. With regards to fibromyalgia, there are deep-set traumas that were probably launched by the subconscious into stimulating the autonomic nervous system. In other words, although one with CFS and FM feels physical pain, its roots may be psychological in nature.

I'm sure that a vast majority of those with chronic fatigue quickly disregard any idea that there might be a link between their physical health problems and their emotional health, but Dr. Sarno argues that when there is no injury to account for someone's pain, there must be another cause, even if it is underlying. He hypothesizes that tension myositis syndrome (TMS) is a mindbody disorder that causes chronic back, neck, and limb pain because tension causes the brain to deprive oxygen to certain areas of the body—such as the muscles of the back.

What Dr. Sarno recommends is that patients consider the physiological basis for TMS and the possible unconscious emotions that might be the underlying cause for their pain. For an excellent explanation of Dr. Sarno's program, watch John Stossel's report on ABC's "20/20" by accessing the following Web site: http://video.google.com/videoplay?docid=-6660313127569317147.

ALTERNATIVE MEDICINE

To me, chronic fatigue syndrome and fibromyalgia are some of the top conditions people are most apt to seek alternative and complementary care for because of the lack of treatments available from the medical community. Because conventional medicine does not have a lot of answers, many flock to alternative remedies such as acupuncture and relaxation techniques, which are purported to stimulate the immune system's production of adenosine triphosphate (ATP), an energy storage compound that the body uses to manufacture antibodies.

In *Alternative Medicine: The Definitive Guide*, William M. Cargile, B.S., D.C. and associated with the American Academy of Oriental Medicine, says he has treated CFS patients using acupuncture alone, concentrating specifically on building the immune system. He does this by using the acupuncture points that relate to autoimmunity and all the meridians (energy channels) in the body.[5]

Some seek relief in herbal remedies. St. John's wort is promoted as a natural alternative to prescription antidepressants. According to Charles Sheperd, M.D., in his book *Living with M.E.: The Chronic/Post-Viral Fatigue Syndrome*, St. John's wort seems to have a lower incidence of side effects than those associated with conventional antidepressant drugs (20 percent versus 60 percent).[6]

Prescription for Nutritional Healing also recommends St. John's wort for its antiviral properties, as well as herbs such as astragalus and echinacea to enhance immune function. Teas brewed from burdock root, dandelion, and red clover enhance immune function as well as cleanse the blood and lymphatic system. If you're more adventurous, try wheatgrass enemas to detoxify the system.[7]

One of the leading alternative medical experts for CFS and FM is Jacob Teitelbaum, M.D., author of *From Fatigued to Fantastic*. He compared our understanding of chronic fatigue and fibromyalgia to the old story of blind men stumbling upon an elephant. One felt the trunk and believed it was a snake. Another felt its leg and thought it was a tree trunk. Another couldn't find the elephant, so he was certain there was nothing there and thought his friends were crazy. "This seems to be the current state of affairs in our understanding of CFS and FM," he wrote.[8]

Dr. Teitelbaum says a good night's sleep is the foundation for getting well (he prefers natural remedies for insomnia, followed by prescription sleep aids). He believes ginger is an herb helpful for pain, as well as capsaicin cream and a supplement known as 5-HTP, which is a form of the amino acid tryptophan. Dr. Teitelbaum also recommends natural remedies such as valerian, glutathione, and St. John's wort.

WHERE WE GO FROM HERE

As someone who has overcome chronic fatigue syndrome and fibromyalgia in my own life, I understand how difficult it is to get a grip on this disease. What I do know is that you're probably sick and tired of being sick and tired, and you would like some spring in your step and some of that old zip back. You'd give anything to wake up in the morning feeling refreshed and pain-free.

Although medical doctors say there is no known cure for chronic fatigue syndrome or fibromyalgia, I believe both conditions are completely reversible through applying the Great Physician's prescription. I recommend a total lifestyle program for the body, mind, and spirit that's based on the seven keys to unlocking your God-given health potential found in my foundational book *The Great Physician's Rx for Health and Wellness*. The Seven Keys are:

- Key #1: Eat to live.

- Key #2: Supplement your diet with whole food nutritionals, living nutrients, and superfoods.

- Key #3: Practice advanced hygiene.

- Key #4: Condition your body with exercise and body therapies.

- Key #5: Reduce toxins in your environment.

- Key #6: Avoid deadly emotions.

- Key #7: Live a life of prayer and purpose.

Each of these keys is part of living a healthy lifestyle and can reduce chronic fatigue and constant pain. I'm one of those who believes that there is a psychological component to CFS and FM, which will be explored further in Key #6: "Avoid Deadly Emotions." You need to make a decided effort to improve both your physical and emotional health if you want to emerge victorious over this illness.

Better health won't happen overnight, but I'm confident the

Great Physician's prescription can work for you because I've met plenty of folks—mostly women—who've told me that the Great Physician's prescription is helping them live the life they've always dreamed of.

I believe each and every one of us has a God-given health potential that can be unlocked, but only with the right keys. I want to challenge you to incorporate these timeless principles and allow God to transform your health as you take on chronic fatigue syndrome and fibromyalgia and reclaim your life.

KEY #1

Eat to Live

M any sufferers from chronic fatigue syndrome and fibromyalgia attempt to change their dietary habits as a way to get some of that old zip back into their lives. They may have heard that certain nutritional deficiencies were contributing to their lackluster energy levels or that following a special diet would allow them to feel like their old selves.

I nod my head in agreement, but only up to a point. According to my research, chronic fatigue syndrome is not strictly a dietary disorder, although you'll find diet-related theories on the causes of CFS or FM, as noted in the Introduction. My view is that following the Great Physician's prescription for eating is vitally important; however, something in the body is obviously not working right, as evidenced by overwhelming fatigue, chronic pain, constant infection, digestive disorders, or liver problems. At the end of the day, there's a strong chance that your body is not working right because you're not *eating* right.

Where diet and CFS and FM intersect is the immune system. Medical physicians believe that an imbalanced immune system is one of the underlying factors contributing to these conditions. When the immune system isn't functioning the way it should, your body fails to eliminate toxins building up in the body. Choosing to eat foods that are part of the Great Physician's prescription sends a battalion of reinforcements to your immune system, providing life-giving nutrients to better deal with toxins leaking from the intestines into the bloodstream and the energy necessary to eliminate these toxins.

Gloria Gilbère, a doctor of naturopathy and natural health, says that leaky gut syndrome (LGS) was the cause of her chronic fatigue and fibromyalgia. She described LGS as something such as a damaged or destroyed digestive filter that allows bacteria, toxins, and foods to leak into the bloodstream. Dr. Gilbère's book, *I Was Poisoned by My Body,* is the first of its kind to connect the causes of autoimmune disorders, allergies, inflammatory diseases, and multiple chemical sensitivities with colon and digestive disorders.

As a CFS and FM sufferer, you probably have a feeling that something isn't right in the digestive tract or that you aren't deriving the energy you need from the foods you eat. When it comes to chronic fatigue syndrome and fibromyalgia, "Your energy level is directly related to the quality of foods you routinely ingest," said Michael Murray, N.D., author of *Healing Foods.*[1]

Tom Cowan, M.D., a San Francisco physician in private practice and columnist on the Weston A. Price Foundation Web site, compared our energy level to a flowing river. "This river has many tributaries or areas to which our energy is diverted," he said. "The main energy 'drain' for most of us is the digestion of our food. When we ease this energy drain going to digesting our food, we suddenly have a huge reserve available for tasks such as muscle function, thinking, exercise, or other more creative pursuits. This is the essence of chronic fatigue syndrome."[2]

Are the foods you're choosing to eat flowing like a river to sustain you, or are they "draining" foods because they're loaded with chemicals and trans-fatty acids, high in sugar, and high in naked calories? Dr. Cowan's point is that eating processed high-starch, low-fiber foods, as well as greasy, fried meats, cause your digestive system to work overtime, leaving your immune system scant amounts of energy available to fight off lingering diseases and conditions.

While managing chronic fatigue syndrome can be as complex as the illness itself, adopting the first key of the Great Physician's prescription—"Eat to Live"—could turn things around in a hurry. This key is founded on two main beliefs:

1. Eat what God created for food.
2. Eat food in a form that is healthy for the body.

Following these two vital principles will give you a great chance to emerge victorious in your quest to get back on the road toward living a healthy, vibrant life.

BACK TO THE SOURCE

What are some foods that God created? My friend Rex Russell, M.D., compiled a comprehensive list in his book *What the Bible Says About Healthy Living* (Regal, 1996). I'm reprinting them here, along with the scriptural references. As you scan through his list, ask yourself if these sound like foods that Moses and the Israelites would have consumed:

- almonds (Gen. 43:11)
- barley (Judg. 7:13)
- beans (Ezek. 4:9)

- bread (1 Sam. 17:17)
- broth (Judg. 6:19)
- cakes (2 Sam. 13:8, and probably not the kind with frosting)
- cheese (Job 10:10)
- cucumbers, onions, leeks, melons, and garlic (Num. 11:5)
- curds of cow's milk (Deut. 32:14)
- figs (Num. 13:23)
- fish (Matt. 7:10)
- fowl (1 Kings 4:23)
- fruit (2 Sam. 16:2)
- game (Gen. 25:28)
- goat's milk (Prov. 27:27)
- grain (Ruth 2:14)
- grapes (Deut. 23:24)
- grasshoppers, locusts, and crickets (Lev. 11:22)
- herbs (Exod. 12:8)
- honey (Isa. 7:15) and wild honey (Ps. 19:10)
- lentils (Gen. 25:34)
- meal (Matt. 13:33 KJV)
- pistachio nuts (Gen. 43:11)
- oil (Prov. 21:17)
- olives (Deut. 28:40)

- pomegranates (Num. 13:23)
- quail (Num. 11:32)
- raisins (2 Sam. 16:1)
- salt (Job 6:6)
- sheep (Deut. 14:4)
- sheep's milk (Deut. 32:14)
- spices (Gen. 43:11)
- veal (Gen. 18:7–8)
- vegetables (Prov. 15:17)
- vinegar (Num. 6:3)[3]

Have these foods been staples in your diet? Do you have to think hard to remember the last time you bit into a fresh apple, scooped up a handful of raisins, or supped on lentil soup? These listed foods are nutritional gold mines and contain no refined or processed carbohydrates and no artificial sweeteners. Since God has given us a bountiful harvest of natural foods to eat, it would take several pages to describe all the fantastic fruits and vibrant vegetables available from His garden. A diet based on whole and natural foods fits within the bull's-eye of eating foods that God created in a form healthy for the body.

I believe God gave us physiologies that crave these foods in their natural state because our bodies are genetically set for certain nutritional requirements by our Creator. Our taste buds, however, have been manipulated by fast-food chains and restaurants that sweeten meats with secret sauces and top everything in sight with melted cheese and bacon. The strategy has worked: we've become a country that loves inexpensive, deep-fried, greasy food. For many of us taste trumps health, which explains why drive-thru chains and sit-down restaurants are doing great business serving cheese-and-egg sandwiches, monster burgers, barrels of fried chicken, and stuffed-crust pizza—foods certainly not in a form that God created.

Having an awareness of what you eat is an important first step to dealing with your chronic fatigue and fibromyalgia. As we begin traveling down this road together, I need to help you understand that everything you eat is a protein, a fat, or a carbohydrate—nutrients that keep the body running at its best. Each of these nutrients positively or negatively affects your digestive tract and your health.

Let's take a closer look at these macronutrients.

The First Word on Protein

Proteins, one of the basic components of foods, are the essential building blocks of the body. All proteins are combinations of twenty-two amino acids, which build body organs, muscles, and nerves, to name a few important duties. Among other things, proteins provide for the transport of nutrients, oxygen, and waste throughout the body and are required for the structure, function, and regulation of the body's cells, tissues, and organs.

Our bodies, however, cannot produce all twenty-two amino acids that we need in order to live a robust life. Scientists have discovered that eight essential amino acids are missing, meaning that they must come from sources outside the body. We need these eight amino acids badly, and it just so happens that animal protein—chicken, beef, lamb, dairy, eggs, and so on—is the only complete protein source providing the Big Eight amino acids.

Chronic fatigue and muscle pain could be due to a deficiency in one or more of the three branch-chain amino acids known as leucine, isoleucine, and valine. This is why I view eating meat (I consider fish or poultry as meats) as essential, because doing so ensures a complete supply of the entire amino acid complex. High-quality eggs and cultured dairy products are also excellent sources of the critical branch-chain amino acids. While plant foods are extremely beneficial for us, they do not contain all the essential amino acids found in animal proteins, which play an important part in retaining muscle strength and keeping your immune system healthy. I'm not in favor of a vegetarian diet when it comes to CFS and FM.

I'm confident that many battling chronic fatigue have been eating the *wrong* kinds of meat for many years. For instance, hamburger is found in every main dish from backyard burgers to spaghetti and meatballs, but in this country the vast majority of hamburger is comprised of ground chuck from hormone-injected cattle who have eaten pesticide-sprayed feed laced with antibiotics.

You would be much better off eating hamburger—as well as other cuts of beef—produced from range-fed and pasture-fed cows. Natural beef is much healthier for you than assembly-line "production" cuts filling our nation's supermarket meat cases. The best and most healthy sources of meat come from organically raised cattle, sheep, goats, buffalo, and venison. Grass-fed beef is leaner and lower in calories than grain-fed beef, and the flavor is tremendous. Organic grass-fed meats are higher in heart-friendly omega-3 fatty acids and important vitamins such as vitamin B_{12}, which is important because a vitamin B_{12} deficiency is thought to be a contributing factor to fatigue.

Another superb protein source is salmon and other cold-water fish, which contain high levels of beneficial essential fatty acids such as omega-3 and omega-6. CFS and FM sufferers have to be careful, however, about eating fish with high mercury levels, which is a toxin associated with fatigue, headaches, depression, and concentration difficulties. You can now find an excellent brand of tuna that is low in mercury and high in omega-3s. I eat this delicious and healthy tuna at least twice per week. (For more information on healthy tuna, visit www.Biblical HealthInstitute.com.)

Also, be careful about purchasing "feedlot salmon" raised on fish farms; they don't compare to their cold-water cousins in terms of taste or nutritional value. While it's great to see more people eating the tender meat of farm-raised Atlantic salmon—albeit colored with orange dye—it's never going to nutritionally match what comes from the wild.

The better alternative is to purchase fresh salmon and other fish from your local fish market or health food store. Look for labels such as "Alaskan" or "wild-caught." Wild-caught fish is an absolutely incredible food and should be consumed liberally. Supermarkets and health food stores are stocking these types of foods in greater quantities these days, and of course, they are found in natural food stores, fish markets, and specialty stores.

THE SKINNY ON FATS

God, in His infinite wisdom, created fats as a concentrated source of energy and source material for cell membranes and various hormones. Fats give foods flavor and aroma by adding creaminess, shine, smoothness, and great mouth feel. In addition, fats are responsible for the regeneration of healthy tissues and maintaining ideal body composition, and they carry the important fat-soluble vitamins A, D, E, and K throughout the body.

Sally Fallon, president of the Weston A. Price Foundation, points out that saturated fatty acids constitute at least 50 percent of all cell membranes, play a vital role in the health of our bones, enhance the immune system, protect the liver from too much alcohol and other toxins, and guard against harmful microorganisms in the digestive tract. For CFS and FM sufferers, the latter is vital because short-chain and medium-chain (saturated) fatty acids protect the intestinal lining, assist in the absorption of nutrients, and properly metabolize carbohydrates. Medium-chain and short-chain fatty acids found in extra virgin coconut oil, palm oil, and butter from grass-fed cows can account for 5 percent to 10 percent of your daily energy requirements.

What type of fats should you eat? The fat found in grass-fed animals, wild-caught fish, free-range poultry, dairy products from grass-fed animals, nuts, seeds, and nut and seed butters are great sources of fats. People are often shocked to hear me say this, but I believe butter is better for you than margarine. Butter, when organically produced, is loaded with healthy fats such as conjugated linoleic acid (CLA) and short-chain saturated fatty acids such as butyric acid, which supply energy to the body and aid in the regeneration of the digestive tract. Margarine, on the other hand, is a man-made, congealed conglomeration of chemicals and hydrogenated liquid vegetable oils loaded with trans fats. I can feel my gut turning sour just at the thought of "buttering" my flaxseed-and-sunflower bread with margarine.

Margarine is just one of today's foods made with hydrogenated fats. Practically every processed food, from Frosted Flakes to Tostitos Tortilla Chips, from Ding Dongs to Dove Bars, contains unhealthy hydrogenated fats and partially hydrogenated fats. These type of fats have been associated with a host of maladies, including diabetes, obesity, and cancer.

The reason food manufacturers use partially hydrogenated oils is to increase shelf life and give flavor stability to foods, but trans fatty acids, or trans fats, are formed when these manufacturers turn these liquid fats into solid fats through hydrogenation. Mark my words: trans fats are bad for you and are found in nearly every processed food stacked on a supermarket shelf: vegetable shortening, crackers, cereals, candies, baked goods, granola bars, snack foods, salad dressings, or anything fried in a restaurant—chicken, steak, or fries.

For years, however, you couldn't find out how much trans fat was in the food you're eating, but that changed in 2006 with the introduction of new Nutrition Facts labels stating the amount of trans fat in the food. The new labeling makes it easier to remove these unhealthy fats from our diets.

Many who suffer from CFS and FM look to low-fat, reduced-fat, or fat-free diets because they've heard that fat is bad for you. Best-selling books such as *The Pritikin Principle* by Nathan Pritikin and *The Ornish Diet* by Dean Ornish, M.D., have preached the gospel of low-fat, high-carbohydrate diets. Around ten years ago, we began seeing supermarket shelves filled with convenience foods displaying the magic words "fat-free" or "reduced fat" on the packaging.

What happened is that consuming low-fat blueberry muffins and reduced-fat ice cream didn't help anyone become healthier. In fact, the case can be argued that the *opposite* happened because, statistically speaking, we've become *fatter* as a nation since the mid-1990s. No one with CFS and FM can say they felt better after snacking on reduced-fat chips and fat-free yogurt.

Generally speaking, low-fat diets have several things working against them. First of all, most people cannot stay on a low-fat regimen for any length of time. "Those who possessed enough will power to remain fat-free for any length of time develop a variety of health problems including low energy, difficulty in concentration, depression, weight gain, and mineral deficiencies," wrote Mary Enig, Ph.D., and Sally Fallon in *Nourishing Traditions.*[4]

In my view, low-fat diets fail to distinguish between the so-called "good fats" in food (including olive and flaxseed oils, tropical oils such as coconut oil, and fish oils) and the "bad fats" (hydrogenated oils found in margarine and most packaged goods). We need certain fats in our diet to provide a concentrated source of energy and source material for cell membranes and various hormones. Fats also provide satiety; without them, we would be hungry within minutes of finishing a meal.

The so-called "bad fats" we don't need are mainly hydrogenated and partially hydrogenated fats found in processed foods, as well as processed vegetable oils such as canola, soy, corn, cottonseed, and safflower oils. (These oils contain high levels of omega-6 fatty acids, which offset the body's natural balance.) Hydrogenated and partially hydrogenated fats are found in sugar-coated flakes for breakfast, a glazed doughnut at break time, fried corn chips and chocolate chip cookies for lunch, and breaded fried chicken nuggets for dinner.

These types of fats aren't good if you're dealing with chronic fatigue and fibromyalgia—or if you're healthy and want to stay that way. The type of fats you do want to consume are:

- omega-3 polyunsaturated fats, such as flaxseed oil and hempseed oil

- monounsaturated (omega-9) fatty acids, such as olive oil, sesame oil, macadamia nut oil, almond oil, and avocado oil

- conjugated linoleic acid (CLA), found in grass-fed meats and dairy products

- healthy saturated fats containing short- and medium-chain fatty acids, such as butter and coconut oil

These good fats are found in a wide range of foods, including salmon, lamb, and goat meat; in dairy products derived from goat's milk, sheep's milk, and cow's milk from grass-fed animals; and in flaxseeds, walnuts, olives, macadamia nuts, and avocados.

The problem with the standard American diet is that people eat too many of the wrong foods containing the wrong fats and not enough of the right foods with the right fats. When it comes to cooking, the top two fats and oils on my list are extra virgin coconut and olive oils, which are beneficial to the body. I urge you to cook with extra virgin coconut oil, which is a near-miracle food that few people have ever heard of.

Coconut oil is packed with antioxidants and reduces the body's need for vitamin E. You can tell which oil is better by comparing how fast canola oil or safflower oil become rancid when sitting at room temperature. Extra virgin coconut oil shows no signs of rancidity even after a year at room temperature.

While oils and foods with trans fat should be eliminated from your diet, I can assure you that fats and oils created by God—as you would expect—are fats you want to include in your diet.

Dealing with Carbs

The third and final macronutrient group is carbohydrates, which, by definition, are the sugars and starches contained in plant foods. While sugars and starches, like fats, are not necessarily bad for you, people with CFS and FM should restrict their consumption of carbohydrates and wisely choose the carbs they eat, because the cravings to eat high-carbohydrate foods will be there.

One of the benefits of reducing the amount of carbohydrates you eat is an improvement in intestinal flora, or bacterial micro-organisms. Few people have heard of intestinal flora or are aware that of the trillions of cells in the human body, 90 percent are found in the large intestine in the form of intestinal flora. The body permits these friendly bacterial to live in the intestinal tract because they are the first line of defense against bacterial diseases, viruses, toxins, and parasites.

The problem with carbohydrates is that the standard American diet is weighted way too heavily on sugar-laden foods. Sugar is a simple carbohydrate that may provide a short-term energy boost, but refined white sugar has a way of feeding the "bad" microorganisms in the intestines. One such organism, a yeast called *Candida albicans*, absolutely *loves* sugar and is thought to contribute heavily to CFS and FM symptoms. Eating too many sugary foods causes Candida (often referred to as "thrush" when the condition becomes pervasive) to thrive, which challenges the immune system and releases toxins into the body. These toxins can cause gas and bloating as well as fatigue and muscle pain.

I recommend that you stay away from eating sugar unnecessarily and cut back on your starches considerably. I will concede that avoiding sugar and its sweet relatives—high fructose corn syrup, sucrose, molasses, and maple syrup—is easier said than done. It's among the first ingredients listed in staples such as cereals, breads, buns, pastries, doughnuts, cookies, ketchup, and ice cream. Many people unwittingly eat sugar with every meal: breakfast cereals are frosted with sugar, break time is soda or coffee mixed with sugar and a Danish, lunch has its cookies and treats, and dinner could be sweet-and-sour ribs topped off with a sugary dessert. But all those sweets can turn your health sour!

You should also cut back on starches such as bread, pasta, and rice (which are known as "complex carbohydrates") because the digestive system finds these type of carbohydrates to be the most difficult to break down. What happens in the digestive process is that some undigested carbohydrates remain in the large intestine and ferment, producing gas and other waste products instead of being properly absorbed and utilized by the body. When unabsorbed carbohydrates camp out in the colon, they feed harmful bacteria and upset the balance of the intestinal flora—a perfect storm for chronic fatigue and fibromyalgia to rear their ugly heads.

The result—gas and acids caused by bacterial fermentation—becomes a vicious cycle, which is why Elaine Gottschall named her book *Breaking the Vicious Cycle*. Unabsorbed carbohydrates encourage bacterial fermentation, and bacterial fermentation makes it more difficult for carbohydrates to be absorbed. As you continue eating high-sugar foods, your body never has a chance to catch up.

You want to consume low-glycemic, high-nutrient, and low-sugar carbohydrates. These would be most high-fiber fruits, especially berries, green vegetables, nuts, seeds, and legumes, plus a small amount of whole grain products, which are always better than refined carbohydrates that have been stripped of their vital fiber, vitamin, and mineral components.

Eating unrefined carbohydrate foods introduces healthy amounts of fiber into your body. Fiber is the indigestible remnants of plant cells found in vegetables, fruits, whole grains, nuts, seeds, and beans. Fiber-rich foods take longer to break down and are partially indigestible, which means that as these foods work their way through the digestive tract, they absorb water and increase the elimination of fecal waste in the large intestine.

Good sources of fiber are berries, fruits with edible skins (apples, pears, and grapes), citrus fruits, whole non-gluten grains (quinoa, millet, amaranth, buckwheat, and brown rice), green peas, carrots, cucumbers, zucchini, tomatoes, and baked or boiled unpeeled potatoes. Green leafy vegetables such as spinach are also fiber-rich. Eating foods high in fiber will immediately improve your blood-sugar levels by slowing the absorption of sugars into your bloodstream.

In summation, it's important to balance proteins, fats, and carbohydrates and to eat high-density but gut-friendly foods with the lowest calories, which will unburden the digestive tract and reduce inflammation, which reduces pain.

Chew on This

You can eat all the right foods in the Great Physician's prescription, but if you're not chewing your food well, then you're a candidate for poor digestion, which is common for folks with CFS and FM. I recommend chewing each mouthful of food twenty-five to fifty times before swallowing. This advice may sound ridiculous, but I know that a conscious effort to chew food slowly ensures that plenty of digestive juices are added to the food as it begins to wind through the digestive tract. I can't emphasize enough the importance of chewing your food well when you're dealing with afflictions such as chronic fatigue and fibromyalgia.

Chewing foods properly allows enzymes in your saliva

to turn the food into a near liquid form before swallowing. Then the mucous in saliva adheres to the food and makes it slippery as it goes down the hatch. One enzyme in saliva, called *salivary amylase*, breaks down carbohydrates. By chewing your food thoroughly, you lower your risk of digestive problems by not sending chunks of food down the gullet. Stomach acids have an easier time breaking down foods that have been properly chewed.

I'm fairly certain that scarfing my meals at Florida State University strongly contributed to my digestive problems. Like most college students, I always ate on the run. A couple of guys in my fraternity were amazed at how fast I could wolf down a meal. "Jordan, you don't eat your food—you swallow it whole," one of them teased.

They wouldn't recognize me at a dinner table today. I've become a much better "chewer"; in fact, if you were to eat out with me sometime, you'd be surprised how long I take to chew my food. It has taken some effort on my part to reprogram the way I eat, yet I know that a conscious effort to chew food slowly ensures that plenty of digestive juices are added to the food as it begins to wind through the digestive tract.

THE TOP HEALING FOODS

I've discussed many healthy foods in this chapter so far, but the following are musts when combating chronic fatigue syndrome and fibromyalgia:

1. **Wild-caught fish.** As mentioned, the omega-3 fatty acids in fish help decrease inflammation. Besides salmon caught in the cold-water Alaskan wilderness, the following fish are high in essential fatty acids: bluefish, capelin, dogfish, herring, mackerel, sardines, anchovies, shad, sturgeon, whitefish, and tuna. Be sure to look for tuna that is low in mercury and high in omega-3 fatty acids. If you're looking to purchase canned tuna, there is now a low-mercury, high omega-3 tuna available that is extremely healthy and safe to consume at the rate of a few cans per week. (See the GPRx Resource Guide at www.Biblical HealthInstitute.com for recommended brands.)

Another type of animal protein I recommend is organically raised, grass-fed cattle, sheep, goats, buffalo, and venison that graze on nature's bountiful pastures. Grass-fed meat is leaner and is lower in calories than grain-fed meat. Organic and grass-fed meats are higher in gut-friendly omega-3 fatty acids and important vitamins such as B_{12} and E.

You should avoid eating certain meats, however. The meats I'm talking about are sausage links, bacon, lunch meats, ham, hot dogs, bratwurst, and other sausages. These meats use preservatives called nitrates to give meats their blood-red color, convey flavor, and resist the development of botulism spores. Nitrates can covert to nitrites, and nitrites have been studied for decades in public and private settings for their ability to cause cancer and tumors in test animals.

I have other reasons for recommending that you stay away from meats such as bacon and ham lunch meat. In all of my previous books, I've consistently pointed out that pork—America's "other white meat"—should be avoided because pigs were called "detestable" and "unclean" in Leviticus and Exodus. God created pigs as scavengers—animals that survive just fine on any farm slop or water swill tossed their way. Pigs have a simple stomach arrangement: whatever a pig eats goes down the hatch, straight into the stomach, and out the back door in four hours max. They'll even eat their own excrement, if hungry enough.

Even if you decide to keep eating commercial beef instead of the organic version, I absolutely urge you to stop eating pork. Read Leviticus 11 and Deuteronomy 14 to learn what God said about eating clean versus unclean animals, where Hebrew words used to describe unclean meats can be translated as "foul" and "putrid," the same terms that describe human waste.

Please realize that not all sea life is healthy to eat, either. Shellfish and fish without fins and scales, such as catfish, shark, and eel, are also described in Leviticus 11 and Deuteronomy 14 as " detestable." God called hard-shelled crustaceans such as lobster, crabs, shrimp, and clams unclean because they are "bottom-feeders," content to sustain themselves on excrement from other fish. To be sure, this purifies water but does nothing for the health of their flesh.

Eating detestable foods fouls the body, and my gut says that's not good for those battling chronic fatigue syndrome and fibromyalgia. God declared these meats detestable and unclean because He understands the ramifications of eating them, and you should as well.

2. **Chicken soup with herbs and spices.** If you're scratching your head, you can stop, because chicken soup is good for the soul. (Wait a minute—that would make a great title to a series

of books!) Stephen Rennard, M.D., chief of pulmonary medicine at the University of Nebraska Medical Center in Omaha,
says that chicken soup acts as an anti-inflammatory because it
apparently reduces the inflammation that occurs when coughs
and congestion strike the respiratory tract.

Dr. Rennard conducted a full-blown study on the medicinal
qualities of chicken soup. He had his wife prepare a batch using
a recipe from her Lithuanian grandmother. Then he carted the
homemade chicken soup to his laboratory, where he combined
some of the soup with neutrophils, or white blood cells, to see
what would happen. As Dr. Rennard suspected, his wife's homemade chicken soup demonstrated that neutrophils showed less
of a tendency to congregate, but at the same time, these neutrophils did not lose any of their ability to fight off germs, which
is a boost for the immune system.[5]

My wife, Nicki, who's a wonderful cook, and I have come up
with an excellent recipe that we call tongue-in-cheek, "CFS- and
FM-Bustin' Chicken Soup." This recipe was inspired by Sally
Fallon, author of *Nourishing Traditions*:

CFS- and FM-Bustin' Chicken Soup

   1 whole chicken (free range, pastured, or organic chicken)
   2–4 chicken feet (optional)
   3–4 quarts cold filtered water
   1 tablespoon raw apple cider vinegar
   4 medium-sized onions, coarsely chopped
   8 carrots, peeled and coarsely chopped
   6 celery stalks, coarsely chopped

2–4 zucchinis, chopped
4–6 tablespoons extra virgin coconut oil
1 bunch parsley
5 garlic cloves
4 inches grated ginger
2–4 tablespoons Celtic Sea Salt
¼–½ teaspoon cayenne pepper

Directions:

If you are using a whole chicken, remove the fat glands and the gizzards from the cavity. By all means, use chicken feet if you can find them. Place chicken or chicken pieces in a large stainless steel pot with the water, vinegar, and all vegetables except parsley. Let stand for ten minutes before heating. Bring to a boil and remove scum that rises to the top. Cover and cook for twelve to twenty-four hours. The longer you cook the stock, the more healing it will be. About fifteen minutes before finishing the stock, add parsley. This will impart additional mineral ions to the broth.

Remove from heat, and take out the chicken and the chicken feet. Let it cool, and remove chicken meat from the carcass, discarding the bones and the feet. Drop the meat back into the soup.

3. **Cultured dairy products from goats, cows, and sheep.** One of the best ways to introduce probiotics to your diet is through cultured dairy products such as yogurt, kefir, hard cheeses, cultured cream cheese, and cottage cheese. Dairy products derived from goat's milk and sheep's milk can be easier on stomachs than those from cows, although dairy products from organic or grass-fed cows

can be excellent as well. Goat's milk and sheep's milk are less allergenic than most cow's milk products because they do not contain the same complex proteins found in cow's milk.

For instance, goat's milk and sheep's milk contain higher amounts of medium-chain fatty acids (MCFAs) than other milks. It's been said that raw or cultured goat's and sheep's milk fully digest in a baby's stomach in just twenty minutes, while pasteurized cow's milk takes eight hours. The difference lies in the goat's milk or sheep's milk structure: their fat and protein molecules are tiny in size, which allows for rapid absorption in the digestive tract.

I believe it's better to drink raw or unpasteurized milk from a certified clean source. Pasteurization kills good as well as harmful bacteria in milk, along with enzymes, making milk harder to digest. This type of milk is available because of improved sanitation methods in the milk-production industry, including the use of stainless steel tanks. Only California and a handful of other states, however, allow raw, unpasteurized milk to be sold. If you happen to live in one of those states, you'll find raw milk to be delicious with a consistency closer to cream.

Those who are lactose-intolerant—and I wager that more than a few with CFS and FM are sensitive to lactose—can often stomach fermented dairy products because they contain little or no residual lactose, which is the type of sugar in milk that many find hard to digest. Sheep and goat's milk are even more digestible because their proteins are easier to break down, contain a little less lactose, and are filled with vitamins, enzymes, and protein. Although goat's milk does have a more pungent smell and taste than cow's milk, sheep's milk tastes just as good as cow's milk. You should be aware that outside the United States, 65 percent of the world's population drink sheep or goat's milk—and they find these milks to be delicious. Goat and sheep cheeses are also wonderful foods to add to your salads.

4. **Cultured and fermented vegetables.** Raw-cultured or fermented vegetables—such as sauerkraut, pickled carrots, beets, or cucumbers—supply the body with probiotics as well. Although these fermented vegetables are often greeted with upturned noses at the dinner table, they help reestablish natural balance to our digestive system. Cultured vegetables such as sauerkraut are brimming with vitamins, such as vitamin C, and contain almost four times the nutrients as unfermented cabbage. The lactobacilli in fermented vegetables contain digestive enzymes that help break down food and increase its digestibility.

Fermentation—the culturing or natural processing of foods with the intentional growth of bacteria, yeast, or mold—has a long history. The Chinese have fermented cabbage for centuries. The Romans also learned to ferment cabbage, or what is known today as "sauerkraut." Eastern Europeans discovered ways to pickle green tomatoes, peppers, and lettuce. Asians became skilled at preparing elaborate fermented foods such as kimchi, a condiment composed of cabbage, other vegetables, and seasonings. And in nearly every culture, dairy products were used to make lacto-fermented foods such as yogurt, kefir, cheese, cottage cheese, and cultured cream (also known as crème fraîche).

The Japanese, who enjoy the longest lifespans in the world and lower rates of heart disease than Americans, eat fermented vegetables such as pickled cabbage, eggplant, and daikon radish with all their traditional meals. I urge you to sample sauerkraut or pickled beets, which are readily available in health food stores.

5. **A wide selections of fruits and vegetables.** The average American consumes far less than the recommended five to nine servings of fruits and vegetables daily, which is a shame. "Some people go through the whole day without eating a single vegetable," states Carolyn Katzin, a nutrition expert at UCLA and a spokeswoman for the American Cancer Society.[6]

I'll settle for something between five and ten servings, which means that instead of reaching for a Danish for a midmorning snack or a candy bar in the afternoon, bite into a banana or a handful of dried apricots. I recommend purchasing organic fruits and veggies, which are loaded with heart-healthy vitamins, minerals, fiber, and antioxidants. Shopping for organically grown fruits and veggies is easier these days since major supermarket chains—even Wal-Mart—are stocking more and more organic fruits and vegetables in their produce departments. Sure, you'll pay anywhere from 10 percent to 100 percent more, but I like to remember this adage: "You can pay the farmer more now, or the doctor more later."

6. **Soaked and sprouted seeds and grains.** When it comes to grain products, seek out items that are "whole grain," which means the bran and germ were left on the grain during processing.

You should say good-bye to white bread, hello to sprouted or sour-leavened whole wheat, rye, or flaxseed breads. Say goodbye to white rice, hello to brown rice and other healthy grains such as amaranth, quinoa, millet, and buckwheat. Say good-bye to pasta made from white enriched flour, hello to sprouted grain or spelt pasta, barley, or couscous.

7. **Nuts.** High-fiber nuts and seeds, even if sprouted, can be difficult to digest. Limit your consumption to two or three ounces a day—and chew well. However, I don't recommend eating cashews and peanuts very often, since they can be more difficult to digest.

8. **Ginger.** The world's most widely cultivated spice, ginger contains chemicals that inhibit toxic bacteria in the digestive tract while it promotes friendly bacteria, which is why this spice is effective in treating digestive conditions ranging from constipation to diarrhea. "Ginger reduces the total volume of gastric juices," says Paul Schulick, author of *Ginger: Common Spice & Wonder Drug*. "From all parts of the world, virtually every ethnomedical text citing ginger has lauded its wide range of benefits to the digestive system," he wrote.[7]

Schulick suggests pouring a cup of boiling water over two tablespoons of freshly grated ginger and letting it steep for five to ten minutes. Then add a dash of hot sauce, or the juice of one lemon, and one to two tablespoons of raw honey, depending on your preferred taste. Sip it throughout the day. Ginger can also be used to season foods.

9. **Water.** Water isn't a food, of course, but this calorie-free and sugar-free substance is vital for the body. F. Batmanghelidj, M.D., author of *You're Not Sick, You're Thirsty!*, said that water is the main

solvent for all foods, vitamins, and minerals. Water breaks down food into smaller particles and helps it metabolize and assimilate. "Water energizes food, and food particles are then able to supply the body with this energy during digestion," he wrote. "This is why food without water has absolutely no energy value for the body."[8]

Dr. Batmanghelidj contends that the brain uses a great deal of electrical energy that is manufactured by what he calls "the water drive of the energy-generating pumps." When you don't drink enough water, the level of energy generation in the brain decreases, which contributes to feelings of the "blahs."

Now is the time for you to set a water bottle on your desk or kitchen counter and to take a sip every ten minutes. You need to drink a minimum of eight glasses of water a day to keep that brain of yours hydrated. Sure, you'll go to the bathroom more often, but is that so bad compared to chronic pain?

I've taken this "drink plenty of water" advice to heart by setting a forty-eight-ounce bottle of water on my office desk as a reminder to keep putting fluids into my system. My one-day record for drinking water is one and one-quarter gallons during a fast, but I won't reveal how many trips I made to the bathroom that day! Drinking water all day long is not only healthy for the body, but it's a key part of the Great Physician's Rx for Chronic Fatigue and Fibromyalgia Battle Plan (see page 75), so keep a water bottle close by and drink water before and during meals.

10. **Apple cider vinegar.** You may have noticed that I included apple cider vinegar in the CFS- and FM-Bustin' Chicken Soup

recipe. There was a reason for that, and it's because I believe apple cider vinegar is an important substance to drink when you're dealing with chronic fatigue and fibromyalgia. One of the beneficial components in apple cider vinegar, especially for those with fibromyalgia, is the high concentration of malic acid, which is believed to help alleviate symptoms of FM.

Apple cider vinegar is made from squeezed liquid of crushed apples. Sugar and yeast are added to the liquid to start the fermentation process, which turns the sugar into alcohol. During a second round of fermentation, the alcohol is converted by acetic acid-forming bacteria into vinegar. The acetic acid is what gives vinegar its sour taste, as well as its minerals: potassium, phosphorus, calcium, magnesium, natural silicon, pectin, and tartaric acids, which help the body maintain its vital acid-alkaline balance. The acidity in apple cider vinegar helps the body rebalance its acid level, which is important as the body tries to find its equilibrium. The icky taste hasn't stopped aficionados from singing the praises of apple cider vinegar, or ACV for short.

Remember: don't drink apple cider vinegar unless it is well diluted. I recommend two to three tablespoons of ACV and one tablespoon of honey mixed in eight to twelve ounces of water; otherwise, you'll be puckering your lips and shaking your head from the tartness of the first sip.

11. **Tea.** Infusions of herbs and spices such as teas have been a part of nearly every culture throughout history. In fact, consuming organic teas and herbal infusions several times per day can be one of the best things you can do for your health. Teas and

herbal infusions can provide energy, enhance the immune system, improve digestion, and provide the body with antioxidants such as polyphenols, which help reduce cellular damage and oxidative stress. Plus, they're a great aid in helping you wind down after a long day!

You'll find in my Great Physician's Rx for Chronic Fatigue and Fibromyalgia Battle Plan (see page 75) that I recommend a cup of hot tea and honey with breakfast, dinner, and snacks. I also advise consuming freshly made iced green tea, as tea can be consumed hot or steeped and iced. Please note that while herbal tea provides many great health benefits, nothing can replace pure water for hydration. Although you can safely and healthfully consume two to four cups per day of tea and herbal infusions, you still need to drink at least six cups of pure water for all the good reasons I've described in this section.

What about Fasting?

If you go to the Web site for the Centers for Disease Control and Prevention (www.cdc.gov) and look into treatment options for chronic fatigue syndrome, you come up with nothing regarding fasting. In fact, the conventional medical community doesn't have much to say about fasting, which I believe is a mistake. I think fasting is extremely beneficial because many of those with chronic fatigue have allergies and could use a break from eating. That's why I'm a firm believer in the value of giving the body time off while your immune system shores up its defenses against strength-sapping invaders and allows the body time to flush out any metal or toxic accumulations.

When I talk about fasting, I think it's better—and more realistic—to concentrate on completing a one-day partial fast once a week, something I do regularly. If you've never voluntarily fasted for a day, I urge you to try it—preferably toward the end of the week. I've found that Thursdays or Fridays work best for me because the week is winding down and the weekend is coming up. For instance, I won't eat breakfast and lunch so that when I break my fast and eat dinner that night, my body has gone between eighteen and twenty hours without food or sustenance since I last ate dinner the night before.

THE DIRTY DOZEN

Here is a list of foods that should never find a way onto your plate or into your hands. I call them "The Dirty Dozen." Some I've already discussed elsewhere in this chapter, while the rest are presented here with a short commentary:

1. **"Unclean" lunch meats and pork products.** These meats top my list because ham, salami, and bacon are staples in the standard American diet and extremely unhealthy.

2. **Shellfish and fish without fins and scales, such as catfish, shark, and eel.** In addition to pork, God called hard-shelled crustaceans such as lobster, crabs, and clams unclean in the Old Testament.

Their flesh harbors known toxins that can contribute to poor health and set your digestive tract on edge. Am I saying au revoir and sayonara to lobster thermidor and shrimp tempura? That's what I'm saying.

3. **Hydrogenated oils.** This means margarine and shortening are taboo, as well as any commercial cakes, pastries, desserts, or products with the words *hydrogenated* or *partially hydrogenated* on the label.

4. **Artificial sweeteners.** Aspartame (found in NutraSweet and Equal), saccharine (Sweet'N Low), and sucralose (Splenda) are chemicals several hundred times sweeter than sugar and found in every sit-down restaurant in America. In my book, artificial sweeteners should be completely avoided whether they come in blue, pink, or yellow packets.

5. **White flour.** White flour isn't a problematic chemical such as artificial sweeteners, but it's virtually worthless and not healthy for you.

6. **White sugar.** If you're looking for another culprit to blame for low energy, then you've found it in white sugar.

7. **Soft drinks.** Run, don't hide, from this liquefied sugar. A twelve-ounce Coke or Pepsi is the equivalent of eating nearly nine teaspoons of sugar. Popular soft drinks also contain chemicals that cause the body to become more acidic, which is not a great feeling for the stomach.

8. **Pasteurized homogenized skimmed milk.** As I said, whole organic cultured milk is better, and goat's milk and sheep's milk are best.

9. **Corn syrup.** Another version of refined sugar and just as bad for you.

10. **Hydrolyzed soy protein.** If you're wondering what in the world this is, hydrolyzed soy protein is found in imitation meat products. Stick to the real stuff.

11. **Artificial flavors and colors.** These are never good for you under the best of circumstances, and certainly not when you're trying to ease digestive pain.

12. **Excessive alcohol.** Long-term, excessive drinking damages every organ in the body (especially the liver), adds weight, produces heart problems, promotes depression, causes digestive problems (ulcers, gastritis, and pancreatitis), and impacts fertility. I must also point out that overconsumption of alcohol has wrecked millions of families over the years.

EAT: WHAT FOODS ARE EXTRAORDINARY, AVERAGE, OR TROUBLE?

I've prepared a comprehensive list of foods that are ranked in descending order based on their health-giving qualities. The best foods to serve and eat are what I call "Extraordinary," foods which God created for us to eat and will give you the best chance to feel peppier. If you are battling chronic fatigue syndrome or fibromyalgia, it's best to consume foods from the Extraordinary category more than 75 percent of the time.

Foods in the Average category should make up less than 25 percent of your daily diet. If you're in the throes of pain or feeling lethargic, consume these foods sparingly.

Foods in the Trouble category should be consumed with extreme caution. If you are dealing with full-blown CFS and FM, you should avoid these foods completely.

For a complete listing of Extraordinary, Average, and Trouble Foods, visit www.BiblicalHealthInstitute.com.

R℞ THE GREAT PHYSICIAN'S Rx FOR CHRONIC FATIGUE AND FIBROMYALGIA: EAT TO LIVE

- *Eat only foods God created.*

- *Eat foods in a form that is healthy for the body.*

- *Consume foods high in omega-3 fatty acids.*

- *Consume foods high in fiber.*

- *Increase consumption of raw fruits and vegetables.*

- *Avoid foods high in sugar.*

- *Avoid foods containing hydrogenated oils.*

- *Consume liberal amounts of homemade chicken soup.*

Take Action

To learn how to incorporate the principles of eating to live into your daily life, turn to page 75 for the Great Physician's Rx for Chronic Fatigue and Fibromyalgia Battle Plan.

KEY #2

Supplement Your Diet with Whole Food Nutritionals, Living Nutrients, and Superfoods

If you were to ask a medical doctor or search the Internet for ways to treat chronic fatigue syndrome and fibromyalgia, you might be advised to take antidepressant drugs or seek out cognitive behavioral therapy, which helps patients cope with illness and develop behaviors that alleviate symptoms. Few conventional medical authorities, however, are willing to champion the idea that taking nutritional supplements is a way to battle these conditions.

I view this cautious reaction as a form of defensive medicine that fails to recognize the enormous potential of nutritional supplements with regards to CFS and FM. I was the beneficiary of a major health turnaround when I was nineteen years old and battling a wide range of ailments, including multiple "incurable" illnesses, severe abdominal cramps, and diarrhea, as well as symptoms of chronic fatigue syndrome and fibromyalgia. My turnaround started when I began taking supplements made with soil-based organisms and other probiotic microorganisms, which are known in the natural health industry as "whole food" or "living" supplements. That's why I'm convinced that nutritional supplements and living nutritionals are an important part of the Great Physician's Rx for Chronic Fatigue and Fibromyalgia Battle Plan (see page 75).

I'll get into details in a moment, but from the outset, please know that I'm not one who believes chronic fatigue and fibromyalgia can be turned around with a bottle of pills. After studying naturopathic medicine and nutrition following my illness, I understand better than most that dietary supplements are just what they say they are—supplements, not a substitute for an inadequate diet, a lack of exercise, or an unhealthy lifestyle.

The basic idea behind nutritional supplements for CFS and FM sufferers is to turn around nutritional deficiencies and strengthen a depleted immune system. To begin with, the CFS and FM sufferer is often low in B vitamins. "The B vitamins act as a team to help speed up chemical reactions and support overall energy metabolism," says *Alternative Medicine: The Definitive Guide*. It continues:

> Since they are essential for red blood cell formation, B complex deficiency produces anemia, the main symptom of which is fatigue. Fatigue and depression have been linked to B-vitamin deficiency. A deficiency of any of the B vitamins also interferes with the immune system's ability to fight disease. Additionally, a New Zealand study found that injection of B_{12} helped normalize imbalances in red blood cells in CFS patients.[1]

B vitamins, including B_2 and B_6, lend support to the nerves and help build reserves of energy. They should be part of a good whole food multivitamin/mineral formula, which contains different compounds such as organic acids, antioxidants, and key nutrients. Whole food multivitamins are more costly to produce since the ingredients—fruits, vegetables, sea vegetables, seeds, spices, vitamins and minerals, etc.—are put through a fermentation process similar to the digestive process of the body, but they are well worth the extra money. A good whole food multivitamin also contains byproducts of probiotic fermentation needed for proper digestion, detoxification, and overall immunity.

Whole food multivitamins contain high concentrations of other minerals and vitamins that should be of benefit:

- Magnesium is crucial for energy production within the cells.

- Vitamin E protects and maintains cellular membranes.

- Vitamin C promotes healthy cell development and is used by the adrenal glands to manufacture stress hormones.

- Compounds of high antioxidant fruits, vegetables, spices, sea vegetables, and tonic mushrooms act as antioxidants, which preserve and protect the body from free radical damage.

Without going into a long explanation, free radicals are something you don't want running rampant within your molecular system. Free radicals are oxygen molecules with a single electron, but these unstable molecules are known to attack the immune system's cells. Antioxidants neutralize free radicals, which is a good thing when you're dealing with an affliction as mysterious as chronic fatigue syndrome or fibromyalgia.

Through scientific research, we've learned that vitamin E is a fat-soluble vitamin present in nuts, seeds, whole grains, apricots, vegetables, and eggs laid by healthy chickens. Vitamin C, chemically known as ascorbic acid, is a water-soluble vitamin present in green peppers, cabbage, spinach, broccoli, kale, cantaloupe, kiwi, strawberries, and citrus fruits and their juices.

Take another look at those foods I just described. Do you think the average person is eating enough of those foods to receive the antioxidants he or she needs? Does a typical American diet of a Danish and coffee for breakfast, hamburger and fries for lunch, and spaghetti and meatballs with garlic bread for dinner fit this bill?

I don't think so, which is why I think everyone needs to take a whole food "living" multivitamin daily—especially folks who are dealing with chronic fatigue and fibromyalgia. Whole food multivitamins provide nutrients that are easy to absorb, which is crucial for CFS and FM patients since digestion is often compromised.

ADAPTOGENIC HERBS

Two herbs worth taking a look into are the eastern Indian herb *Ashwaghandha* and the Russian herb *Rhodiola rosea*. Ashwaghandha root has been used for centuries in Ayurvedic medicine, the traditional medicine system originating in India. Rhodiola rosea, also known as Golden Root, is a perennial plant that grows in dry sandy ground at high altitudes in the arctic areas of Europe and Asia. This herb has been used in Russian traditional medicine for relieving anxiety and depression.

Ashwaghandha and Rhodiola rosea are adaptogens, which are endurance enhancers. In various research studies, Ashwaghandha and Rhodiola rosea, when mixed into hot water as tea or taken in extract form as a nutritional supplement, have been found to:

- benefit overall health
- control stress-related weight gain
- revitalize metabolic processes associated with restlessness and fatigue
- promote emotional well being
- regulate and balance body organs for increased physical and mental rejuvenation
- support blood sugar and cholesterol levels already within the normal range

Prescription for Natural Cures recommends that those with chronic fatigue syndrome should take Ashwaghandha (either as a tea or in a supplement form) daily as a tonic for fatigue and anxiety.[2]

MEDICINAL OR TONIC MUSHROOMS

I've written fourteen books in the Great Physician's Rx series, but this is the first time I've specifically recommended medicinal or tonic mushrooms, which are tailor-made for CFS and FM symptoms.

During my studies in naturopathic medicine, I learned about the body's immune system components and natural methods of improving immune function, which is key for sufferers of chronic fatigue and fibromyalgia. I found that certain compounds in edible fungi enhance the production of cytokines, which are immune-cell secretions that facilitate cell-to-cell communication and fully optimize immune function.

I would imagine that right about now you're scratching your head over the phrase "edible fungi." What I'm referring to are mushrooms, which have been used for centuries in the Orient to maintain health and increase stamina and longevity. Although the healing aspects of mushrooms have been passed down through folklore, medical researchers have been studying the healing properties of mushrooms for the last twenty to thirty years.

Mushrooms such as cordyceps, ganoderma (reishi), coriolus, maitake, and shiitake have tremendous potential and are well worth adding to your supplemental program.

PROBIOTICS AND DIGESTIVE ENZYMES

Probiotics in dietary supplement form are a great way to reintroduce beneficial microorganisms into your digestive tract, which can improve bowel and immune system function, increase nutrient absorption, and detoxify the body and its organs. I think the best probiotics are the ones that contain lactic-acid bacteria, soil-based organisms, and beneficial yeasts, which are room-temperature stable and do not require refrigeration as most common probiotic supplements do.

Digestive enzymes are complex proteins involved in the digestive process. I always make sure I take a couple of digestive enzymes before I dig into a meal at home and especially on the road. Let me explain why: when we eat raw foods such as salad and fruit, we consume the enzymes they contain, which aids in the digestion of the salad or fruit. When we eat cooked or processed meals, as in a restaurant, however, the body's pancreas must produce the enzymes necessary to digest them. The constant demand for enzymes strains the pancreas, which must kick in more enzymes to keep up with the demand. Without the proper levels of enzymes from foods—either raw or fermented—or by taking digestive enzymes in supplement form, you are susceptible to excessive gas and bloating, diarrhea, constipation, heartburn, and low energy, which has become the typical postmeal experience for too many Americans these days.

Enzymes are complex proteins involved in the digestive process. They are the body's laborers, the ones responsible for synthesizing, delivering, and eliminating the unbelievable number of ingredients and chemicals that your body uses during the waking hours. When the body produces enzymes, their job is to stimulate chemical changes in the foods passing through the gut. The pancreas, which takes a lead role in producing digestive enzymes for the body, has to keep up by producing pancreatic enzymes.

Junk-food diets, fast chewing, and eating on the run contribute to the body's inability to produce adequate enzyme production and the subsequent malabsorption of food. These problems get worse as we age, not better. Dr. Edward Howell, a leading biochemist, cited numerous animal studies in his book *Enzyme Nutrition*, showing that animals that were fed diets deficient in enzymes experienced enlargements of the pancreas because the organs were working overtime to produce digestive enzymes. It wasn't long before their health was severely affected.

One should eat raw food in its natural, unprocessed state more often, but there are times when it isn't always possible, as I can attest when I travel or have a heavy social schedule. But the last thing you want to eat when you have digestive problems is fried food, because items such as fried chicken and French fries must be cooked in oil at higher temperatures than the boiling point, which damages fats and destroys all enzymes.

So, if you're having trouble finding a way to eat enough raw, fresh foods such as salad greens, bananas, avocados, seeds, nuts, grapes, and other natural foods, then take plant-based digestive enzymes to improve your digestion each time you eat. Digestive enzymes are available at your local natural food store, and you can find recommended brands by visiting www.BiblicalHealth Institute.com and clicking on the GPRx Resource Guide.

Omega-3 Cod Liver Oil

One of my favorite supplements is omega-3 cod liver oil, which contains high concentrations of omega-3 fatty acid, which seems to improve mood (due to omega-3s), reduce inflammation (due to omega-3s and vitamin D), and enhance the immune system (due to vitamin A). Vitamin A is depleted during post-viral syndromes, which some people believe is involved with chronic fatigue syndrome.

I added omega-3 cod liver oil to my daily diet ten years ago when I was in the midst of my recovery. I recommend taking between one teaspoon and one tablespoon of omega-3 cod liver oil each day to receive those much-needed omega-3 fatty acids. Sure, you may have to hold your nose to swallow this supplement known for its fishy odor and taste, but there are some excellent brands that come in lemon, mint, and other flavors. You can also take this important nutrient in easy-to-swallow liquid capsules.

THE GREAT PHYSICIAN'S RX FOR CHRONIC FATIGUE AND FIBROMYALGIA: SUPPLEMENT YOUR DIET WITH WHOLE FOOD NUTRITIONALS, LIVING NUTRIENTS, AND SUPERFOODS

- *Take whole food living multivitamins with each meal.*

- *Add the adaptogenic herbs Ashwaghandha and Rhodiola rosea to your daily regimen.*

- *Consume daily medicinal or tonic mushrooms that have gone through a fermentation process.*

- *Take omega-3 cod liver oil with dinner each day.*

- *Use digestive enzymes and probiotics to improve digestion and elimination*

Take Action

To learn how to incorporate the principals of supplementing your diet with whole food nutritionals, living nutrients, and superfoods into your daily lifestyle, please turn to page 75 for the Great Physician's Rx for Chronic Fatigue and Fibromyalgia Battle Plan.

KEY #3

Practice Advanced Hygiene

I will be the first to admit that dipping your face into a basin of facial solution, cleaning under your fingernails with a special soap, or washing your hands after going to the bathroom doesn't sound as if it has as much to do with chronic fatigue syndrome or fibromyalgia. But there's an aspect to good hygiene that's relevant to this discussion, and it has to do with inflammation.

First, a little high-school biology lesson.

Every day of your life, your body wards off gazillions of germs, which break down your immune system and make you more susceptible to health problems. Every *other* day of your life (or so it seems), little "ow-ees" happen: a stubbed toe, mosquito bite, slight sunburn, pulled muscle, or nick while shaving. Whenever any of these scenarios happen, the body mounts an instantaneous defense, sending cells and natural chemicals to assault those nasty flu germs or repair the slight gash in your skin. Scientifically speaking, this response is known as *inflammation*.

Most people think inflammation is something that happens to your back after digging up weeds all Saturday morning. Actually, inflammation occurs internally as well. When viruses invade the respiratory system or you wolf down a hot dog from the street vendor, the body launches a counterattack that lays waste to outside intruders or repairs any infected bodily organs.

When inflammation occurs, the liver produces a protein known as high-sensitivity C-reactive protein. This natural chemical is released into the bloodstream to help the body fight flu germs, for example, or repair itself after you pull a splinter out of your index finger. What medical researchers are learning, however, is that chronic fatigue syndrome may be caused by inflammation of pathways in the nervous system, according to the NIH.[1]

This is noteworthy because Key #3 of *The Great Physician's Rx for Chronic Fatigue and Fibromyalgia,* "Practice Advanced Hygiene," can protect your body from becoming chronically inflamed, which will lower your C-reactive protein levels as well as lower your risk of developing CFS and FM—or at least the likelihood of exacerbating their symptoms. There is growing evidence that an imbalanced immune system and stress from environmental toxins and germs are factors in CFS and FM, which underscores the importance of advanced hygiene.

So, what do I mean by the phrase "advanced hygiene"?

I'm glad you asked. I'm a great believer in protecting myself from harmful germs, and I've been practicing an advanced hygiene protocol for more than a decade. I've witnessed the results in my own life: no lingering head colds, no nagging sinus infections, and no acute respiratory illnesses to speak of for many years.

I follow a program first developed by an Australian scientist, Kenneth Seaton, Ph.D., who discovered that ear, nose, throat, and skin problems could be linked to the fact that humans touch their noses, eyes, and mouths with germ-carrying fingernails throughout the day. In scientific terms, this is known as auto- or self-inoculation. And how do your fingernails get dirty? Through hand-to-hand contact with surfaces and other people—

by shaking hands with others or touching things they touched: handrails, doorknobs, shopping carts, paper money, coins, and food. If you thought that most germs were spread by airborne exposure—someone sneezing at your table, for example—you would be wrong. "Germs don't fly, they hitchhike," Dr. Seaton declared, and he's right.

Dr. Seaton estimates that once you pick up hitchhiking germs, they hibernate and hide around the fingernails, no matter how short you keep them trimmed. You would be surprised to find out how frequently you itch your nose or rub your mouth and eyes; if you're like most people, it's a constant habit. When you come into contact with contagious germs, you can get sick, come down with the common cold, or find yourself battling the flu. This happens all too often. Chuck Gerba, a University of Arizona environmental-microbiology professor, says that 80 percent of infections, from cold and flu viruses to food-borne diseases, are spread through contact with hands and surfaces.[2]

I know this isn't pleasant dinner conversation, but practicing advanced hygiene has become an everyday habit for me. Since I'm aware that 90 percent of germs take up residence around my fingernails, I use a creamy semisoft soap rich in essential oils. Each morning and evening I dip both of my hands into the tub of semisoft soap and dig my fingernails into the cream. Then I work the special cream around the tips of my fingers, cuticles, and fingernails for fifteen to thirty seconds. When I'm finished, I rinse my hands under running water, lathering them for fifteen seconds before rinsing. After my hands are clean, I take another dab of semisoft soap and wash my face.

My next step involves a procedure that I call a "facial dip." I fill my washbasin or a clean large bowl with warm but not hot water. When enough water is in the basin, I add one to two tablespoons of regular table salt and two eyedroppers of a mineral-based facial solution into the cloudy water. I mix everything up with my hands, and then I bend over and dip my face into the cleansing matter, opening my eyes several times to allow the membranes to be cleansed. After coming up for air, I dunk my head a second time and blow bubbles through my nose. "Sink snorkeling," I call it.

My final two steps of advanced hygiene involve the application of very diluted drops of hydrogen peroxide and minerals into my ears for thirty to sixty seconds to cleanse the ear canal, followed by brushing my teeth with an essential oil tooth solution to cleanse my teeth, gums, and mouth of unhealthy germs. (For more information on my favorite advanced hygiene products, visit www.BiblicalHealthInstitute.com and click on the GPRx Resource Guide.)

Brushing your teeth well and regularly practicing advanced hygiene involves discipline; you have to remind yourself to do it until it becomes an ingrained habit. I find it easier to follow these steps in the morning when I'm freshly awake than later in the evening when I'm tired and bleary-eyed—although I do my best to practice advanced hygiene morning and evening and hardly ever miss. Either way, I know it only takes three minutes or so to complete all of the advanced hygiene steps, and those might be the best three minutes of your day for overall health.

A Primer on Washing Your Hands

1. Wet your hands with warm water. It doesn't have to be close to scalding hot.

2. Apply plenty of soap into the palms of both hands. The best soap to use is a semisoft soap into which you can dig your fingernails.

3. Rub your hands together vigorously, and scrub all the surfaces. Pay attention to the skin between the fingers, and work the soap into the fingernails.

4. Rub and scrub for fifteen to thirty seconds, or about the time it takes to slowly sing "Happy Birthday."

5. Rinse well and dry your hands on a paper towel or clean cloth towel. If you're in a public restroom, it's a good idea to turn off the running water with the towel in your hand. An even *better* idea is to use that same towel to open the door, since that door handle is the first thing that nonwashers touch after they've gone to the bathroom.

6. Keep waterless sanitizers in your purse or wallet in case soap and water are not available in the public restroom. These solutions, although not ideal, are better than nothing.

When to Wash Your Hands

- after you go to the bathroom
- before and after you insert or remove contact lenses
- before and after food preparation
- before you eat
- after you sneeze, cough, or blow your nose
- after cleaning up pet messes
- after handling money
- after changing a diaper
- after wiping a child's nose
- after handling garbage
- after cleaning your toilet
- after shaking hands
- after shopping at the supermarket
- after attending an event at a public theater
- before and after sexual intercourse

THE GREAT PHYSICIAN'S RX FOR CHRONIC FATIGUE AND FIBROMYALGIA: PRACTICE ADVANCED HYGIENE

- *Dig your fingers into a semisoft soap with essential oils and wash your hands regularly, paying special attention to removing germs from underneath your fingernails.*

- *Cleanse your nasal passageways and the mucous membranes of the eyes daily by performing a facial dip.*

- *Cleanse the ear canals at least twice per week.*

- *Use an essential oil–based tooth solution daily to remove germs from the teeth, gums, and mouth.*

Take Action

To learn how to incorporate the principles of practicing advanced hygiene into your daily lifestyle, please turn to page 75 for the Great Physician's Rx for Chronic Fatigue and Fibromyalgia Battle Plan.

Key #4

Condition Your Body
with Exercise and Body Therapies

Feeling tired?

I thought so. Fatigue and weakness are constant companions for those suffering from chronic fatigue syndrome and fibromyalgia. When you add the mental, emotional, and spiritual stresses that come from dealing with around-the-clock weariness, even the act of getting off the couch can be too much to physically ask for.

CFS and FM sufferers often feel lethargic when they wake up and lack energy to do anything throughout the day. Many are bedridden. Because they don't—or can't—maintain a normal, physical lifestyle during their waking hours, their muscles atrophy and their movements slow down like an Energizer Bunny who can't bang the drum any longer. They lack the vigor to pull themselves out of the downward spiral.

For many of those with CFS and FM, learning to manage activity levels is key to managing their condition. This requires a new way of defining exercise. For instance, while vigorous aerobic classes can be beneficial, many CFS patients don't have the energy to complete an hour-long class. It's asking too much of their bodies.

I was a certified personal trainer in my early twenties, so I would suggest "functional fitness"—a form of gentle exercise that's easy on your body, gets you burning calories, and improves agility, to people who suffer from CFS and FM but want to exercise. The idea behind functional fitness is to train movements, not muscles, as you build up cardiovascular endurance and the body's core muscles. You do this through performing real-life activities in real-life positions.

Functional fitness employs your own body weight as resistance, but you can also utilize dumbbells, mini-trampolines, and stability balls. Classes in functional fitness are gaining popularity around the country. Instructors at LA Fitness, Bally Total Fitness, and local YMCAs put you through a series of exercises that mimic movements from everyday life. You're asked to perform squats with feet apart, with feet together, and with one foot back and the other forward. You're asked to do reaching lunges, push-ups against a wall, and "supermans," which involve lying on the floor and lifting up your right arm while lifting your left leg into a fully extended position. You're not asked to perform high-impact, fatiguing exercises such as those found in energetic, pulsating aerobics classes. (For more information on functional fitness, visit www.BiblicalHealthInstitute.com.)

Even if you lack the energy to exercise, your body's joints, cartilage, ligaments, muscles, bones, and tendons need to be used! I understand that you may not feel like getting out of bed when you have CFS and FM, but if you can do some stretching and flexibility exercises, which are the core of functional fitness, you'll be much better off. Even if the last time you exercised was when President Bill Clinton was making his morning jogs to McDonald's, I urge you to start exercising again, because movement and physical activity are fundamental keys to good health.

If you're looking for a different form of low-impact exercise, try jumping on rebounders, which look like mini-trampolines. One optimal rebounding session can cause a gentle but energized fatigue that revitalizes the lungs and the body's cells. According to Morton Walker, D.P.M. and author of *Jumping for Health*, each gentle bounce pits sixty trillion body cells against the earth's gravitational pull. This interaction strengthens every cell in the body while saving strain on your muscles and joints. The result, says Dr. Walker, is better health with less exertion.

Walking is another gentle exercise that's tailor made for those who feel they lack the energy even to try functional fitness. This low-impact exercise places a gentle strain on the hips and the rest of the body. When done briskly, walking makes the heart work harder and strengthens little-used muscles. Best of all, you can walk when it fits your schedule—before work, on your lunch hour, before dinner, or after dinner. You set the pace; you decide how much you put into this exercise. Walking is also a great social exercise that allows you to carry on a civilized conversation with a friend or loved one.

Finally, another form of body therapy that's popular in the CFS and FM community is swimming laps or taking part in water aerobics classes. Standing in neck-deep water cancels out about 90 percent of your body weight, which greatly reduces stress on your weight-bearing joints and allows you to gently exercise your limbs and raise your heart rate. Since most pools are treated with chlorine, which can be toxic to the body, I encourage you to swim in the ocean or a pool that utilizes salt water purification.

The Wonders of Hydrotherapy

Hydrotherapy is a fifty-cent word meaning "to use water to heal in various ways," and I think water can do a world of good for those dealing with chronic fatigue. Baths, showers, steam rooms, saunas, washings, wraps, and hot tubs are forms of hydrotherapy, which is probably the easiest and least physically demanding way to experience some measure of relief from CFS and FM symptoms.

Soaking in a tub or standing under a strong spray of steamy hot water facilitates muscle relaxation and decreases joint pain and stiffness, but be careful with saunas because they could wear you out. Taking baths with essential oils such as myrtle, coriander, hyssop, galbanum, or frankincense gives you an opportunity to practice hydrotherapy and aromatherapy at the same time. A few drops of these essential oils in a hot bath could have a significant impact on how you feel.

Another great way to detoxify the body of harmful environmental chemicals, fat soluble toxins, and heavy metals is the regular use of a far infrared sauna. Far infrared saunas provide a comfortable and simple way to improve health while gently raising the heart rate, and regular users have reported an improvement in skin tone and a lessening of aches and pains. I have owned and used a far infrared sauna for more than eight years and highly recommend it. (For more information on far infrared sauna technology, visit www.BiblicalHealthInstitute.com.)

A hydrotherapy favorite of mine involves the therapeutic qualities of hot and cold showers. Cold water stimulates the body and boosts oxygen use in the cells. Hot water dilates blood vessels, which improves blood circulation, speeds the elimination of toxins, and transports more oxygen to the brain. After I take a hot shower, I switch off the hot water and allow my skin to be blasted by freezing cold water for sixty seconds. That'll get you going in the morning!

LET THE SUN SHINE IN

My next body therapy may sound really off-the-wall to you, but get some sun during the day. You heard me right, even though we've all heard about the dangers of developing skin cancer from sunbathing on the beach. The truth is we need more sun, not less, because the body miraculously synthesizes the ultraviolet rays of the sun into vitamin D, which plays a vital role in immunity and blood cell formation as well as in fighting infection.

Dr. Joe Mercola, on his Web site, mercola.com, said that studies have found low vitamin D may contribute to chronic fatigue.[1] The reason I'm making a big deal about sunlight and vitamin D is that vitamin D is not a true vitamin but a critical hormone that helps regulate the health of more than thirty different tissues and organs, from the brain to the kidneys. Vitamin D plays a role in regulating cell growth, the immune system, and blood pressure; your body needs this vital hormone. If you're dealing with low energy and chronic fatigue, one of the healthier activities you can do is sit in a chair, close your eyes, and take deep breaths with a bright sun beating down on you.

I urge you to get some sunshine once or twice a day, but try to avoid the hours between ten o'clock in the morning and two o'clock in the afternoon. The NIH says all you need is ten to fifteen minutes of sunlight for vitamin D synthesis to occur.

SLEEP AND REST

If you have chronic fatigue syndrome or fibromyalgia, chances are that you don't wake up feeling refreshed. Those with CFS and FM have trouble staying in the deep, restorative stages of sleep that recharge the batteries. Poor sleep can cause immune suppression, which can lead to a host of other maladies.

Sleep is a body therapy in short supply these days. A nationwide "sleep deficit" means that we're packing in as much as we can from the moment we wake up until we crawl into bed sixteen, seventeen, or eighteen exhausting hours later. American adults are down to a little less than seven hours of sleep each night, a good two hours less than our great-great-grandparents slept a hundred years ago.

How many hours of sleep are you getting nightly? The magic number is eight hours, say the sleep experts. That's because when people are allowed to sleep as much as they would like in a controlled setting, such as in a sleep laboratory, they naturally sleep eight hours in a twenty-four-hour time period.

It's easy for me to sit back and say, "Just get more sleep," when it comes to fighting chronic fatigue. What I've found most beneficial is following the advice of Dr. Mercola, who told me that one hour of sleep *before* midnight is equal to four hours of sleep after midnight. I know he is right because when I go to bed really late, say around two o'clock in the morning, I don't feel well when I wake. But when I go to bed before midnight, I wake up refreshed and ready to hit the day. If you've been a night owl, try going to bed an hour or two before midnight and see what difference it makes in your life.

In addition to proper sleep, the body needs a time of rest every seven days to recharge its batteries. This is accomplished by taking a break from the rat race on Saturday or Sunday. God created the earth and the heavens in six days and rested on the seventh, setting an example for us and a reminder that we need to take a break from our labors. Otherwise, we're prime candidates for wearing ourselves out.

So try to fall asleep before midnight, and take it easy on the weekend.

R︮X THE GREAT PHYSICIAN'S RX FOR CHRONIC FATIGUE SYNDROME AND FIBROMYALGIA: CONDITION YOUR BODY WITH EXERCISE AND BODY THERAPIES

- *Make a commitment and an appointment to exercise at least three times a week.*

- *Incorporate five to fifteen minutes of functional fitness into your daily schedule.*

- *Take a brisk walk and see how much better you feel at the end of the day.*

- *End each shower by changing the water temperature to cool (or cold) and standing underneath the spray for one minute.*

- *Go to sleep earlier, paying close attention to how much sleep you get before midnight. Do your best to get eight hours of sleep nightly. Remember that sleep is the most important nonnutrient you can incorporate to improve your health.*

- *Once each day, sit outside in a chair and face the sun. Soak up the rays for ten or fifteen minutes.*

- *Next Saturday or Sunday, take a day of rest. Dedicate the day to the Lord and do something fun and relaxing that you haven't done in a while. Make your rest day work-free, errand-free, and shop-free. Trust God that He'll do more with His six days than you can do with seven.*

Take Action

To learn how to incorporate the principles of conditioning your body with exercise and body therapies into your daily lifestyle, please turn to page 75 for the Great Physician's Rx for Chronic Fatigue Syndrome and Fibromyalgia Battle Plan.

KEY #5

Reduce Toxins in Your Environment

M any theories are floating out there about what causes chronic fatigue and fibromyalgia. Some say that people with chronic fatigue can't get rid of a viral infection. Others believe they are infected with yeast such as candida, which challenges the immune system and releases toxins into the body, resulting in fatigue and muscle pain. Some believe parasites damage the lining of the gut, causing all sorts of digestive mischief: gas, bloating, poor digestion, and infrequent elimination. Hidden food allergies and sensitivities can set off symptoms of feeling tired all the time. Others say people experience unrelenting fatigue because one or more of their endocrine glands, such as the thyroid, doesn't produce enough hormones. Still others believe that an overabundance of heavy metals such as mercury, cadmium, and lead can be a contributor to these diseases.

My friend, Don Colbert, M.D., author of *What You Don't Know May Be Killing You,* suffered from symptoms of chronic fatigue and jaundice after his dental fillings leaked mercury into his bloodstream. For decades, dentists have filled cavities with amalgam, which is a mixture of silver, tin, copper, zinc, and mercury. When fillings crack and leak, minute concentrations of mercury become absorbed by the body, potentially causing all sorts of havoc. Dr. Colbert, who took the unusual step of having his old fillings removed and replaced on his road to recovery, described in his book the specifics of how mercury poisons different systems in the body.

The US Department of Health and Human Services studied the amalgam filling issue in the 1990s and concluded that "there is scant evidence that the health of the vast majority of people with amalgam is compromised or that removing fillings has a beneficial effect on health."[1] A follow-up study by the American Dental Association reported that "no health consequences from exposure to such low levels of mercury released from amalgam restorations have been demonstrated."[2]

It's beyond the scope of this book to fully explore the issue of amalgam fillings vis-à-vis chronic fatigue and fibromyalgia, but I will say this: if you had your blood and urine tested for various chemicals and toxins inside your body, you'd be in for a big surprise: lab technicians would likely uncover dozens of toxins in your bloodstream, including PCBs (polychlorinated biphenyls), dioxins, furans, trace metals, phthalates, VOCs (volatile organic compounds), and chlorine. Scientists refer to this chemical residue as a person's *body burden.*

Although our bodies are designed to eliminate toxins, our immune systems have become overloaded because of the chemicals and other toxins present in the foods we eat, the air we breathe, and the water we drink. Some toxins are water-soluble, meaning they are rapidly passed out of the body and present no harm. Unfortunately, many more toxins are fat soluble, meaning that it can take months or years before they are completely eliminated from our systems.

I could fill this entire book about the toxins in the foods we eat, but Russell L. Blaylock, M.D., has already done it. In his book *Excitotoxins: The Taste That Kills*, he explains how monosodium glutamate (MSG), hydrolyzed vegetable protein, aspartame, aspartate, and other chemicals found in our foods are examples of excitotoxins, which are substances that over-excite neurons to the point of cell damage and, eventually, cell death. Food manufacturers add these chemicals, Dr. Blaylock said, because they stimulate the taste cells in the tongue, thereby enhancing the taste of the food. Now you know why advertising for a national brand of potato chips says, "Bet you can't eat just one."

If you're dealing with chronic fatigue and fibromyalgia, you must pay close attention to eliminating toxins from your body. A good place to start is by eliminating all processed foods from your diet and eating as healthily and organically as possible. You should only consume organic and grass-fed meat and dairy products, since most commercially produced beef, chicken, and pork act as chemical magnets for toxins in the environment. You should increase the fiber in your diet in order to eliminate toxins through the bowel, exercise and sweat to eliminate toxins through the lymphatic system, and practice deep breathing to eliminate toxins through the lungs.

What to Drink

I've already touted the healthy benefits of drinking water in Key #1, but when it comes to reducing toxins in your environment, water is especially important because of its ability to flush out toxins and other metabolic wastes from the body. The importance of drinking enough water cannot be overstated when you're dealing with chronic fatigue: water is a life force involved in nearly every bodily process, from digestion to blood circulation. Your heart pumps blood much more efficiently when you're well hydrated because the blood is thinner. You're not going to feel as tired when you're drinking the proverbial eight glasses of water daily.

I know what you're thinking: *Jordan, if I drink that much water, I can never be further than fifteen steps from a bathroom.* Yes, you will probably triple your trips to the toilet, but trust me on this: if you're serious about doing something about your chronic fatigue and fibromyalgia, you must be serious about drinking enough water. There's no better physiological way for you to rid yourself of chemicals and toxins stored inside your body.

I don't recommend drinking water straight from the tap, however. Nearly all municipal water is routinely treated with chlorine or chloramine, potent bacteria-killing chemicals. I've installed a whole-house filtration system that removes the chlorine and other impurities out of the water *before* it enters our household pipes. My wife, Nicki, and I can confidently turn on the tap and enjoy the health benefits of chlorine-free water for drinking, cooking, and bathing. Since our water doesn't have a chemical aftertaste, we're more apt to drink it.

When I'm at the office or out and about, I sip on bottled water all day long. My feelings are that given a choice, you're better off purchasing bottled water from a natural spring source, although filtered tap water (Dasani and Aquafina, for example) would be okay too. My favorite bottled water brands are Mountain Valley Spring Water, Volvic Natural Spring Water, Trinity Springs Water, and Nariwa Water. All of these bottled waters come from natural springs and are highly beneficial to the body. (For more information on my favorite bottled waters, see the GPRx Resource Guide, which can be found at www.BiblicalHealthInstitute.com.)

Toxins Elsewhere in Your Environment

There are other toxins in your home or immediate environment that may not be directly related to chronic fatigue and fibromyalgia but are important enough to mention since they are detrimental to health:

- **Household cleaners.** Many of today's commercial house cleaners contain potentially harmful chemicals and solvents that expose people to VOCs (volatile organic compounds), which can cause eye, nose, and throat irritation.

   Nicki and I have found that natural ingredients such as vinegar, lemon juice, and baking soda are excellent substances that make our home spick-and-span. Natural cleaning products that aren't harsh, abrasive, or potentially dangerous to your family are available in grocery and natural food stores.

- **Skin-care and body-care products.** Toxic chemicals such as chemical solvents and phthalates are found in lipstick, lip gloss, lip conditioner, hair coloring, hair spray, shampoo, and soap. Ladies, when you rub a tube of lipstick across your lips, your skin readily absorbs these toxins, and that's unhealthy. As with household cleaners, you can find natural cosmetics in natural food markets and progressive grocery stores, although they are becoming more widely available in drug stores and beauty stores.

- **Toothpaste.** A tube of toothpaste contains a warning that in case of accidental swallowing you should contact the local Poison Control Center. What's that all about? Most commercially available toothpastes contain artificial sweeteners, potassium nitrate, sodium fluoride, and a whole bunch of long, unpronounceable words. Again, search out a healthy, natural version.

THE GREAT PHYSICIAN'S RX FOR CHRONIC FATIGUE AND FIBROMYALGIA: REDUCE TOXINS IN YOUR ENVIRONMENT

- *Eat organic meat from organically produced, grass-fed sources to lower your exposure to environmental toxins.*

- *When eating canned fish, look for low-mercury, high omega-3 sources of tuna.*

- *Drink the recommended eight glasses of water daily— or one quart for every fifty pounds of body weight.*

- *Use glass containers instead of plastic containers whenever possible.*

- *Improve indoor air quality by opening windows or buying an air filtration system.*

- *Use natural cleaning products for your home.*

- *Use natural products for skin care, body care, hair care, cosmetics, and toothpaste.*

Take Action

To learn how to incorporate the principles of reducing toxins in your environment, please turn to page 75 for the Great Physician's Rx for Chronic Fatigue and Fibromyalgia Battle Plan.

KEY #6

Avoid Deadly Emotions

Medical professionals in the conventional and alternative fields agree that chronic fatigue syndrome is a complicated illness characterized by at least six months of extreme fatigue. According to Harvard Medical School, about half of those with chronic fatigue develop depression in the months and years after the condition begins. "However, available evidence indicates that chronic fatigue syndrome is not a psychiatric illness," said Harvard doctors. "Rather, it appears to be a physical illness that *leads* to depression in some people" (italics added for emphasis).[1]

Makes sense to me. Pain and fatigue can lay anyone down low, so dealing with chronic aches and constant lethargy can be downright depressing. Many with chronic fatigue and fibromyalgia wonder if they will *ever* feel like their old selves, which is a natural reaction.

Although most cases of chronic fatigue and fibromyalgia are not life-threatening, that doesn't lessen the impact of missing activities you once enjoyed or the freedom of movement to which you'd grown accustomed. Perhaps you lack the energy to enjoy skiing, hitting tennis balls, or chasing a little white ball around a golf course. Maybe you find hiking or even walking too much of a chore. No one feels chipper about facing an uncertain future with chronic fatigue and fibromyalgia.

When it comes to the role of deadly emotions and CFS and

FM, how you feel emotionally affects how you feel physically, and the opposite is also true. According to Don Colbert, M.D., author of the book, *Deadly Emotions*, researchers have directly and scientifically linked emotions to diseases related to the immune system, which would include chronic fatigue and fibromyalgia.[2]

If you're bottling up emotions such as anger, bitterness, or resentment regarding your chronic fatigue, these deadly emotions will produce toxins similar to bingeing on a dozen glazed doughnuts. The efficiency of your immune system decreases noticeably for six hours, which can knock you down even lower. Staying angry and bitter about how sick you feel can even prompt you to fall off the healthy food wagon. An old proverb states it well: "What you are eating is not nearly as important as what's eating you."

I've heard a great deal about an interesting emotional health program outlined in *A More Excellent Way: Be in Health—Spiritual Roots of Disease, Pathways to Wholeness,* by Henry Wright, a pastor in Thomaston, Georgia. The author maintains that 80 percent of all illnesses have spiritual roots. Regarding chronic fatigue syndrome, he made this observation: "Chronic fatigue is the first part of the name of the disease. The symptoms are exhaustion, lethargy, lack of motivation, and lack of energy flow. The word 'syndrome' basically means they don't know what causes it. When you hear the word 'incurable' or 'unknown' with 'syndrome,' you usually have a spiritually rooted disease."[3]

I don't have the space available to delve into Pastor Wright's statements in greater depths, but I urge you to check out his book if you think you need to be freed from some past trauma, sin, or bitter spiritual root in your life. If that's not possible, speak with a counselor, your pastor, or trusted and loyal friends. Don't forget that God promises to forgive all our sins and heal all our diseases (Psalm 103:3).

EMOTIONAL PAIN TOO

If you are in the midst of health challenges, deadly emotions can quickly deplete your dwindling reserves of energy and strength, especially if you are still dealing with depression and anger issues.

One of the deadliest of all emotions is unforgiveness. Perhaps you've had a traumatic experience or suffered great emotional pain from someone in the past. Are there people who've hurt you so badly that you can't find it in your heart to forgive them? It's a question worth pondering, because I believe an unforgiving heart is an underlying factor in many health problems, including chronic fatigue syndrome and fibromyalgia.

Please remember that no matter how bad you've been hurt in the past, it's still possible to forgive. "For if you forgive men their trespasses, your heavenly Father will also forgive you," Jesus said. "But if you do not forgive men their trespasses, neither will your Father forgive your trespasses" (Matt. 6:14–15 NKJV).

We've been talking about negative emotions and their effects on the body, but the flip side of the coin is that positive emotions such as love, acceptance, and laughter are a fragrant balm to the soul. "A merry heart doeth good like a medicine," says Proverbs 17:22 (KJV), and a jolt of humor could allow you to forget—at least momentarily—what's ailing you.

If you're angry, hurt, or bothered by those who've been mean to you, give them your forgiveness, and then let it go.

Start a Small Group

It's difficult to deal with chronic fatigue and fibromyalgia alone. If you have friends or family members who are struggling, ask them to join you in following the Great Physician's Rx 7 Weeks of Wellness small group program. To learn about joining an existing group in your area or leading a small group in your church, please visit www.BiblicalHealthInstitute.com.

℞ THE GREAT PHYSICIAN'S RX FOR CHRONIC FATIGUE AND FIBROMYALGIA: AVOID DEADLY EMOTIONS

- *Simplify your life, and do your best to avoid stress, anxiety, and anger.*

- *Trust God when you face circumstances that cause you to worry or become anxious.*

- *Forgive those who have hurt you, and see how God can heal when you forgive.*

- *Look for ways to laugh; it's your best medicine (Proverbs 17:22).*

Take Action

To learn how to incorporate the principles of avoiding deadly emotions into your daily regimen, please turn to page 75 for the Great Physician's Rx for Chronic Fatigue and Fibromyalgia Battle Plan.

KEY #7

Live a Life of Prayer and Purpose

The path that chronic fatigue syndrome and fibromyalgia take is much like the path that a hurricane takes: unpredictable. Most of the time, CFS and FM don't travel in a straight path, meaning that people often experience periods of illness as well as periods of relative well-being.

The long-term outlook is also unpredictable. Sometimes people recover within a year; sometimes it's several years. Sometimes people recover to a point where they can resume work and other "normal" activities even as they continue to experience periodic symptoms. Some individuals with severe cases never recover. Also, God may not choose to physically heal someone with chronic fatigue syndrome or fibromyalgia. The affliction becomes their "thorn in the flesh," as Paul described in 2 Corinthians 12: 7–9 (NKJV):

And lest I should be exalted above measure by the abundance of the revelations, a thorn in the flesh was given to me, a messenger of Satan to buffet me, lest I be exalted above measure. Concerning this thing I pleaded with the Lord three times that it might depart from me. And He said to me, "My grace is sufficient for you, for My strength is made perfect in weakness." Therefore most

71

gladly I will rather boast in my infirmities, that the power
of Christ may rest upon me.

While physical health isn't the most important thing in the
grand scheme of things—I believe a relationship with a living
God is—the fact of the matter is that spiritual health and physical health are closely linked. The good news is that chronic fatigue
syndrome and fibromyalgia are both completely reversible, and
my great encouragement to you—the reader—is to believe that
and fight for your life.

Each of the 7 Keys can directly support your desire to tri-
umph over chronic fatigue and fibromyalgia, and I believe each
and every one of us has a God-given health potential that can
be unlocked only with the right keys. I'm asking you to incorporate these timeless principles and allow the living God to
transform your health as you honor Him with your body as a
living sacrifice, as it says in Romans 12:1 (NIV): "Therefore, I
urge you, brothers, in view of God's mercy, to offer your bodies as living sacrifices, holy and pleasing to God—this is your
spiritual act of worship."

We all have a purpose in life, and while that purpose may be
clouded by years of physical illness, God is not done with you
yet. If you say to yourself, *I'm not sure I have a purpose,* you
would be wrong. If there is breath in your lungs, you have a purpose; it's ingrained in your being.

If you haven't found your purpose yet, search your heart.
What makes you feel alive? What are you passionate about?

The joys of family? The arts? Teaching others? Your purpose is waiting to be discovered. Pinpoint your passions, and you'll uncover your purpose. Keep in mind that God gives us different desires, different dreams, and different talents because we are all part of one body. Having a purpose will give you something to live for.

OUR PIPELINE TO GOD

In living a healthy, purpose-filled life, prayer is the most powerful tool that we possess. Prayer connects the entire person—body, mind, and spirit—to God. Through prayer, God takes away our guilt, shame, bitterness, and anger and gives us a brand-new start. We can eat organic whole foods, supplement our diet with whole food supplements, practice advanced hygiene, reduce toxins, and exercise, but if our relationship is not where it needs to be with God, then we will never be completely healthy. Talking to our Maker through prayer is the foundation for optimal health and makes us whole. After all, God's love and grace are our greatest foods for mind, body, and spirit.

The seventh key to unlocking your health potential is living a life of prayer and purpose. Prayer will confirm your purpose, and it will give you the perseverance to complete it. Seal all that you do with the power of prayer, and watch your life become more than you ever thought possible.

R℞ THE GREAT PHYSICIAN'S RX FOR CHRONIC FATIGUE AND FIBROMYALGIA: LIVE A LIFE OF PRAYER AND PURPOSE

- *Pray continually.*

- *Confess God's promises upon waking and before you retire.*

- *Find God's purpose for your life and live it.*

- *Reach out to someone you know who needs this message and share it.*

Take Action

To learn how to incorporate the principles of living a life of prayer and purpose into your daily life, please turn to page 75 for the Great Physician's Rx for Chronic Fatigue and Fibromyalgia Battle Plan.

THE GREAT PHYSICIAN'S RX
FOR CHRONIC FATIGUE AND
FIBROMYALGIA BATTLE PLAN

DAY 1

Upon Waking

Prayer: thank God because this is the day the Lord has made. Rejoice and be glad in it. Thank Him for the breath in your lungs and the life in your body. Ask the Lord to heal your body and use your experience to benefit the lives of others. Read Matthew 6:9–13 aloud.

Purpose: ask the Lord to give you an opportunity to add significance to someone's life today. Watch for that opportunity. Ask God to use you this day for His intended purpose.

Advanced hygiene: for hands and nails, press fingers into semisoft soap four or five times, and lather hands with soap for fifteen seconds, rubbing soap over cuticles and rinsing under water as warm as you can stand. Take another swab of semisoft soap into your hands and wash your face. Next, fill a basin or sink with water as warm as you can stand, and add one to three tablespoons of table salt and one to three eyedroppers of iodine-based mineral solution. Dunk face into water and open eyes, blinking repeatedly underwater. Keep eyes open underwater for three seconds. After cleaning your eyes, put your face back in the water, and close your mouth while blowing bubbles out of your nose. Come up from the water, and immerse your face in the water once again, gently taking water into your nostrils and expelling bubbles. Come up from the water, and blow your nose into facial tissue. To cleanse the ears, use hydrogen peroxide and mineral-based ear drops, putting two or three drops into each ear and letting stand for sixty seconds. Tilt your head to expel the drops. For the teeth, apply two or three drops of essential-oil-based tooth drops to the toothbrush. This can be used to brush your teeth or added to existing toothpaste. After brushing your teeth, brush your tongue for fifteen seconds. (For recommended advanced hygiene products, visit www.Biblical HealthInstitute.com and click on the Resource Guide.)

Reduce toxins: open your windows for one hour today. Use natural soap and natural skin- and body-care products (shower gel, body creams, etc.). Use natural facial-care products. Use natural toothpaste. Use natural hair-care products such as shampoo, conditioner, gel, mousse, and hairspray. (For recommended products, visit www.BiblicalHealth Institute.com and click on the Resource Guide.)

Morning supplements: make a drink with one tablespoon of raw organic apple cider vinegar and two teaspoons of raw organic honey dissolved in twelve ounces of warm purified water. Drink with two capsules of a systemic enzyme blend with proteases, bromelain, and papain. (For recommended products, visit www.BiblicalHealthInstitute.com and click on the Resource Guide.)

Body therapy: get twenty minutes of direct sunlight sometime during the day, but be careful between ten o'clock in the morning and two o'clock in the afternoon.

Exercise: begin by performing functional fitness exercises for five minutes or spend five minutes on a mini-trampoline. Finish with five minutes of deep-breathing exercises. Caution: the following exercises are designed to be gentle on the body and should be energizing—not draining. If you are suffering from extreme fatigue, please start slowly. (One to three rounds of the exercises can be found at www.BiblicalHealthInstitute.com.)

Emotional health: whenever you face a circumstance, such as your health, that causes you to worry, repeat the following: "Lord, I trust You. I cast my cares upon You, and I believe that You're going to take care of [insert your current situation] and cause me to be in good health and make my body strong." Confess that throughout the day whenever you think about your health condition.

Breakfast

Make a smoothie in a blender with the following ingredients:

1 cup organic plain yogurt or kefir (sheep's milk is best)

1 tablespoon organic flaxseed oil

1–2 tablespoons raw organic honey

1 cup of organic fruit (berries, banana, peaches, pineapple, etc.)

2 tablespoons goat's milk protein powder (for recommended brands, visit www.BiblicalHealthInstitute.com and click on the Resource Guide)

dash of vanilla extract (optional)

Supplements: take one capsule of whole food probiotic formula with soil-based organisms, one capsule of an immune system support formula with tonic mushrooms, and one capsule of an adaptogenic herbal blend with B vitamins. (For recommended brands, visit www.BiblicalHealth Institute.com and click on the Resource Guide.)

Lunch

Before eating, drink eight ounces of water.

During lunch, drink eight ounces of water, or hot or iced green tea with honey.

large green salad with mixed greens, avocado, carrots, tomato, red cabbage, red onions, red peppers, and sprouts with three hard-boiled omega-3 eggs

salad dressing: mix extra virgin olive oil, apple cider vinegar or lemon juice, minced fresh garlic, naturally brewed soy sauce, Celtic sea salt, herbs, and spices together; or, mix one tablespoon of extra virgin olive oil with one tablespoon of a healthy store-bought dressing

one apple with skin

Supplements: take one capsule of whole food probiotic formula with soil-based organisms, one capsule of an immune system support formula with tonic mushrooms, and one capsule of an adaptogenic herbal blend with B vitamins.

Dinner

Before eating, drink eight ounces of water.

During dinner, drink hot or iced green tea with honey. (For recommended brands, visit www.BiblicalHealthInstitute.com and click on the Resource Guide.)

baked, poached, or grilled wild-caught salmon

steamed broccoli

large green salad with mixed greens, avocado, carrots, cucumbers, celery, tomato, red cabbage, red onions, red peppers, and sprouts

salad dressing: mix extra virgin olive oil, apple cider vinegar or lemon juice, minced fresh garlic, naturally brewed soy sauce, Celtic sea salt, herbs, and spices together; or, mix one tablespoon of extra virgin olive oil with one tablespoon of a healthy store-bought dressing

Supplements: take one capsule of whole food probiotic formula with soil-based organisms, one capsule of an immune system support formula with tonic mushrooms, and one capsule of an adaptogenic herbal blend with B vitamins and one–to three teaspoons or three to nine capsules of a high omega-3 cod liver oil complex. (For recommended brands, visit www.BiblicalHealthInstitute.com and click on the Resource Guide.)

Snacks

Drink eight to twelve ounces of water, or hot or iced green tea with honey. (for recommended brands, visit www.BiblicalHealth Institute.com and click on the Resource Guide.)

apple slices with raw almond butter

one berry antioxidant whole food nutrition bar with beta-glucans from soluble oat fiber (for recommended brands, visit www.Biblical HealthInstitute.com and click on the Resource Guide)

Before Bed

Exercise: go for a short walk outdoors, weather permitting, or on an indoor treadmill.

Supplements: make a drink with one tablespoon of raw organic apple cider vinegar and two teaspoons of raw organic honey dissolved in twelve ounces of warm purified water. Drink with two capsules of a systemic enzyme blend with proteases, bromelain, and papain.

Body therapy: take a warm bath for fifteen minutes with eight drops of biblical essential oils added.

Advanced hygiene: repeat the advanced hygiene instructions from the morning.

Emotional health: ask the Lord to bring to your mind someone you need to forgive. Take a sheet of paper and write the person's name at the top. Try to remember each specific action that person did against you that brought you pain. Write the following: "I forgive [insert person's name] for [insert the action he or she did against you]." After you fill the paper, tear it up or burn it, and ask God to give you the strength to truly forgive that person.

Purpose: ask yourself these questions: "Did I live a life of purpose today?" "What did I do to add value to someone else's life today?" Commit to living a day of purpose tomorrow.

Prayer: thank God for this day, asking Him to give you a restoring night's rest and a fresh start tomorrow. Thank Him for His steadfast love that never ceases and His mercies that are new every morning. Read Romans 8:35, 37–39 aloud.

Sleep: go to bed by half past ten.

DAY 2

Upon Waking

Prayer: thank God because this is the day that the Lord has made. Rejoice and be glad in it. Thank Him for the breath in your lungs and the life in your body. Ask the Lord to heal your body and use your experience to benefit the lives of others. Read Psalm 91 aloud.

Purpose: ask the Lord to give you an opportunity to add significance to someone's life today. Watch for that opportunity. Ask God to use you this day for His intended purpose.

Advanced hygiene: follow the advanced hygiene recommendations from the morning of Day 1.

Reduce toxins: follow the recommendations to reduce toxins from the morning of Day 1.

Morning supplements: make a drink with one tablespoon of raw organic apple cider vinegar and two teaspoons of raw organic honey dissolved in twelve ounces of warm purified water. Drink with two capsules of a systemic enzyme blend with proteases, bromelain, and papain.

Body therapy: take a hot-and-cold shower. After a normal shower, alternate sixty seconds of water as hot as you can stand it, followed by sixty seconds of water as cold as you can stand it. Repeat cycle four times for a total of eight minutes, finishing with cold water.

Exercise: begin by performing functional fitness exercises for five minutes or spend five minutes on a mini-trampoline. Finish with five minutes of deep-breathing exercises. Caution: the following exercises are designed to be gentle on the body and should be energizing—not draining. If you are suffering from extreme fatigue, please start slowly. (One to three rounds of the exercises can be found at www.BiblicalHealth Institute.com.)

Emotional health: follow the emotional health recommendations from the morning of Day 1.

Breakfast

two or three omega-3 eggs any style, cooked in one tablespoon of extra virgin coconut oil (for recommended brands, visit www.Biblical HealthInstitute.com and click on the Resource Guide)

stir-fried onions, garlic, mushrooms, and peppers

one slice of sprouted or yeast-free whole grain bread with almond butter and honey

Supplements: take one capsule of whole food probiotic formula with soil-based organisms, one capsule of an immune system support formula with tonic mushrooms, and one capsule of an adaptogenic herbal blend with B vitamins.

Lunch

Before eating, drink eight ounces of water.

During lunch, drink eight ounces of water, or hot or iced green tea with honey.

large green salad with mixed greens, avocado, carrots, tomato, red cabbage, red onions, red peppers, and sprouts, adding two ounces of low-mercury, high omega-3 tuna (for recommended brands, visit www.BiblicalHealthInstitute.com and click on the Resource Guide)

salad dressing: mix extra virgin olive oil, apple cider vinegar or lemon juice, minced fresh garlic, naturally brewed soy sauce, Celtic sea salt, herbs, and spices together; or, mix one tablespoon of extra virgin olive oil with one tablespoon of a healthy store-bought dressing

organic dark grapes (preferably with seeds)

Supplements: take one capsule of whole food probiotic formula with soil-based organisms, one capsule of an immune system support formula with tonic mushrooms, and one capsule of an adaptogenic herbal blend with B vitamins.

Dinner

Before eating, drink eight ounces of water.

During dinner, drink hot or iced green tea with honey.

roasted organic chicken

cooked vegetables (carrots, onions, garlic, peas, etc.)

large green salad with mixed greens, avocado, carrots, tomato, red cabbage, red onions, red peppers, and sprouts salad dressing: mix extra virgin olive oil, apple cider vinegar or lemon juice, minced fresh garlic, naturally brewed soy sauce, Celtic sea salt, herbs, and spices together; or, mix one tablespoon of extra virgin olive oil with one tablespoon of a healthy store-bought dressing

Supplements: take one capsule of whole food probiotic formula with soil-based organisms, one capsule of an immune system support formula with tonic mushrooms, one capsule of an adaptogenic herbal blend with B vitamins, and one to three teaspoons or three to nine capsules of a high omega-3 cod liver oil complex.

Snacks

Drink eight to twelve ounces of water, or hot or iced green tea with honey.

one cup of organic berries

one berry antioxidant whole food nutrition bar with beta-glucans from soluble oat fiber

Before Bed

Exercise: go for a walk outdoors, weather permitting, or walk on an indoor treadmill.

Supplements: make a drink with one tablespoon of raw organic apple cider vinegar and two teaspoons of raw organic honey dissolved in twelve ounces of warm purified water. Drink with two capsules of a systemic enzyme blend with proteases, bromelain, and papain.

Advanced hygiene: repeat the advanced hygiene instructions from the morning of Day 1.

Emotional health: repeat the emotional health recommendations from Day 1.

Purpose: ask yourself these questions: "Did I live a life of purpose today?" "What did I do to add value to someone else's life today?" Commit to living a day of purpose tomorrow.

Prayer: thank God for this day, asking Him to give you a restoring night's rest and a fresh start tomorrow. Thank Him for His steadfast love that never ceases and His mercies that are new every morning. Read 1 Corinthians 13:4–8 aloud.

Body therapy: spend ten minutes listening to soothing music before you retire.

Sleep: go to bed by half past ten.

DAY 3

Upon Waking

Prayer: thank God because this is the day the Lord has made. Rejoice and be glad in it. Thank Him for the breath in your lungs and the life in your body. Ask the Lord to heal your body and use your experience to benefit the lives of others. Read Ephesians 6:13–18 aloud.

Purpose: ask the Lord to give you an opportunity to add significance to someone's life today. Watch for that opportunity. Ask God to use you this day for His intended purpose.

Advanced hygiene: follow the advanced hygiene recommendations from the morning of Day 1.

Reduce toxins: follow the recommendations to reduce toxins from the morning of Day 1.

Morning supplements: make a drink with one tablespoon of raw organic apple cider vinegar and two teaspoons of raw organic honey dissolved in twelve ounces of warm purified water. Drink with two capsules of a systemic enzyme blend with proteases, bromelain, and papain.

Body therapy: get twenty minutes of direct sunlight sometime during the day, but be careful between ten o'clock in the morning and two o'clock in the afternoon.

Exercise: begin by performing functional fitness exercises for five minutes or spend five minutes on a mini-trampoline. Finish with five minutes of deep-breathing exercises. Caution: the following exercises are designed to be gentle on the body and should be energizing—not draining. If you are suffering from extreme fatigue, please start slowly. (One to three rounds of the exercises can be found at www.BiblicalHealth Institute.com.)

Emotional health: follow the emotional health recommendations from Day 1.

Breakfast

Drink one cup of hot or iced green tea with honey.

four to eight ounces of organic whole milk yogurt or cottage cheese with fruit (pineapple, peaches, or berries), one teaspoon of raw organic honey, one teaspoon of flaxseed oil, and a dash of vanilla extract

handful of raw almonds

Supplements: take one capsule of whole food probiotic formula with soil-based organisms, one capsule of an immune system support formula with tonic mushrooms, and one capsule of an adaptogenic herbal blend with B vitamins.

Lunch

Before eating, drink eight ounces of water.

During lunch drink eight ounces of water, or hot or iced green tea with honey.

large green salad with mixed greens, avocado, carrots, tomato, red cabbage, red onions, red peppers, and sprouts, adding three hard-boiled omega-3 eggs

salad dressing: mix extra virgin olive oil, apple cider vinegar or lemon juice, minced fresh garlic, naturally brewed soy sauce, Celtic sea salt, herbs, and spices together; or, mix one tablespoon of extra virgin olive oil with one tablespoon of a healthy store-bought dressing

organic grapes or berries

Supplements: take one capsule of whole food probiotic formula with soil-based organisms, one capsule of an immune system support formula with tonic mushrooms, and one capsule of an adaptogenic herbal blend with B vitamins.

Dinner

Before eating, eight ounces of water.

During dinner, drink hot or iced green tea with honey.

red meat steak (beef, buffalo, or venison)

steamed broccoli

baked sweet potato with butter

large green salad with mixed greens, avocado, carrots, tomato, red cabbage, red onions, red peppers, and sprouts

salad dressing: mix extra virgin olive oil, apple cider vinegar or lemon juice, minced fresh garlic, naturally brewed soy sauce, Celtic sea salt, herbs, and spices together; or, mix one tablespoon of extra virgin olive oil with one tablespoon of a healthy store-bought dressing

Supplements: take one capsule of whole food probiotic formula with soil-based organisms, one capsule of an immune system support formula with tonic mushrooms, one capsule of an adaptogenic herbal blend with B vitamins, and one to three teaspoons or three to nine capsules of a high omega-3 cod liver oil complex.

Snacks

Drink eight to twelve ounces of water, or hot or iced green tea with honey.

healthy chocolate (cacao) snack (for recommended brands, visit www.BiblicalHealthInstitute.com and click on the Resource Guide)

one whole food nutrition bar with beta-glucans from soluble oat fiber

Before Bed

Exercise: go for a short walk outdoors, weather permitting, or on an indoor treadmill.

Supplements: make a drink with one tablespoon of raw organic apple cider vinegar and two teaspoons of raw organic honey dissolved in twelve ounces of warm purified water. Drink with two capsules of a systemic enzyme blend with proteases, bromelain, and papain.

Body therapy: take a warm bath for fifteen minutes with eight drops of biblical essential oils added.

Advanced hygiene: follow the advanced hygiene instructions from the morning of Day 1.

Emotional health: follow the forgiveness recommendations from the evening of Day 1.

Purpose: ask yourself these questions: "Did I live a life of purpose today?" "What did I do to add value to someone else's life today?" Commit to living a day of purpose tomorrow.

Prayer: thank God for this day, asking Him to give you a restoring night's rest and a fresh start tomorrow. Thank Him for His steadfast love that never ceases and His mercies that are new every morning. Read Philippians 4:4–8, 11–13,19 aloud.

Sleep: go to bed by half past ten.

DAY 4

Upon Waking

Prayer: thank God because this is the day the Lord has made. Rejoice and be glad in it. Thank Him for the breath in your lungs and the life in your body. Read Matthew 6:9–13 aloud.

Purpose: ask the Lord to give you an opportunity to add significance to someone's life today. Watch for that opportunity. Ask God to use you this day for His intended purpose.

Advanced hygiene: follow the advanced hygiene recommendations from Day 1.

Reduce toxins: follow the recommendations for reducing toxins from Day 1.

Morning supplements: make a drink with one tablespoon of raw organic apple cider vinegar and two teaspoons of raw organic honey dissolved in twelve ounces of warm purified water. Drink with two capsules of a systemic enzyme blend with proteases, bromelain, and papain.

Exercise: begin by performing functional fitness exercises for five minutes or spend five minutes on a mini-trampoline. Finish with five minutes of deep-breathing exercises. Caution: the following exercises are designed to be gentle on the body and should be energizing—not draining. If you are suffering from extreme fatigue, please start slowly. (One to three rounds of the exercises can be found at www.Biblical HealthInstitute.com.)

Body therapy: take a hot and cold shower. After a normal shower, alternate sixty seconds of water as hot as you can stand it, followed by sixty seconds of water as cold as you can stand it. Repeat cycle four times for a total of eight minutes, finishing with cold.

Emotional health: follow the emotional health recommendations from the morning of Day 1.

Breakfast

Drink one cup of hot or iced green tea with honey.

three soft-boiled or poached omega-3 eggs

four ounces of sprouted whole grain cereal with two ounces of whole milk yogurt or sheep's milk. (for recommended brands, visit www.Biblical HealthInstitute.com and click on the Resource Guide)

Supplements: take one capsule of whole food probiotic formula with soil-based organisms, one capsule of an immune system support formula with tonic mushrooms, and one capsule of an adaptogenic herbal blend with B vitamins.

Lunch

Before eating, drink eight ounces of water.

During lunch, drink eight ounces of water, or hot tea with honey.

large green salad with mixed greens, avocado, carrots, tomato, red cabbage, red onions, red peppers, and sprouts, adding two ounces of low mercury, high omega-3 tuna

salad dressing: mix extra virgin olive oil, apple cider vinegar or lemon juice, minced fresh garlic, naturally brewed soy sauce, Celtic sea salt, herbs, and spices together; or, mix one tablespoon of extra virgin olive oil with one tablespoon of a healthy store-bought dressing

one bunch of organic dark grapes (preferably with seeds)

Supplements: take one capsule of whole food probiotic formula with soil-based organisms, one capsule of an immune system support formula with tonic mushrooms, and one capsule of an adaptogenic herbal blend with B vitamins.

Dinner

Before eating, drink eight ounces of water.

During dinner, drink hot tea with honey.

grilled chicken breast

steamed veggies

small portion of cooked whole grain (quinoa, amaranth, millet, or brown rice) cooked with 1 tablespoon of extra virgin coconut oil

large green salad with mixed greens, avocado, carrots, tomato, red cabbage, red onions, red peppers, and sprouts

salad dressing: mix extra virgin olive oil, apple cider vinegar or lemon juice, minced fresh garlic, naturally brewed soy sauce, Celtic sea salt, herbs, and spices together; or, mix one tablespoon of extra virgin olive oil with one tablespoon of a healthy store-bought dressing

Supplements: take one capsule of whole food probiotic formula with soil-based organisms, one capsule of an immune system support formula with tonic mushrooms, one capsule of an adaptogenic herbal blend with B vitamins, and one to three teaspoons or three to nine capsules of a high omega-3 cod liver oil complex.

Snacks

Drink eight to twelve ounces of water, or hot or iced green tea with honey.

apple and carrots with raw almond butter

one berry antioxidant whole food nutrition bar with beta glucans from soluble oat fiber

Before Bed

Drink eight to twelve ounces of water, or hot or iced green tea with honey.

Exercise: go for a short walk outdoors, weather permitting, or walk on an indoor treadmill.

Supplements: make a drink with one tablespoon of raw organic apple cider vinegar and two teaspoons of raw organic honey dissolved in twelve ounces of warm purified water. Drink with two capsules of a systemic enzyme blend with proteases, bromelain, and papain.

Advanced hygiene: follow the advanced hygiene recommendations from the morning of Day 1.

Emotional health: follow the forgiveness recommendations from the evening of Day 1.

Purpose: ask yourself these questions: "Did I live a life of purpose today?" "What did I do to add value to someone else's life today?" Commit to living a day of purpose tomorrow.

Prayer: thank God for this day, asking Him to give you a restoring night's rest and a fresh start tomorrow. Thank Him for His steadfast love that never ceases and His mercies that are new every morning. Read Romans 8:35, 37–39 aloud.

Body therapy: spend ten minutes listening to soothing music before you retire.

Sleep: go to bed by half past ten.

DAY 5 (PARTIAL FAST DAY)

Upon Waking

Prayer: thank God because this is the day the Lord has made. Rejoice and be glad in it. Thank Him for the breath in your lungs and the life in your body. Read Isaiah 58:6–9 aloud.

Purpose: ask the Lord to give you an opportunity to add significance to someone's life today. Watch for that opportunity. Ask God to use you this day for His intended purpose.

Advanced hygiene: follow the advanced hygiene recommendations from Day 1.

Reduce toxins: follow the recommendations for reducing toxins from Day 1.

Morning supplements: make a drink with one tablespoon of raw organic apple cider vinegar and two teaspoons of raw organic honey dissolved in twelve ounces of warm purified water. Drink with two capsules of a systemic enzyme blend with proteases, bromelain, and papain.

Exercise: begin by performing functional fitness exercises for five minutes or spend five minutes on a mini-trampoline. Finish with five minutes of deep-breathing exercises. Caution: the following exercises are designed to be gentle on the body and should be energizing—not draining. If you are suffering from extreme fatigue, please start slowly. (One to three rounds of the exercises can be found at www.BiblicalHealth Institute.com.)

Body therapy: get twenty minutes of direct sunlight sometime during the day, but be careful between the hours of ten o'clock in the morning and two o'clock in the afternoon.

Emotional health: follow the emotional health recommendations from the morning of Day 1.

Breakfast

Drink eight to twelve ounces of water.

no food (partial-fast day)

Lunch

Drink eight to twelve ounces of water.

no food (partial-fast day)

Dinner

Before eating, drink eight ounces of water.

During dinner, drink hot or iced green tea with honey.

chicken soup (visit www.GreatPhysiciansRx.com for the recipe)

cultured vegetables (for recommended brands, visit www.Biblical HealthInstitute.com and click on the Resource Guide)

large green salad with mixed greens, avocado, carrots, tomato, red cabbage, red onions, red peppers, and sprouts

salad dressing: mix extra virgin olive oil, apple cider vinegar or lemon juice, minced fresh garlic, naturally brewed soy sauce, Celtic sea salt, herbs, and spices together; or, mix one tablespoon of extra virgin olive oil with one tablespoon of a healthy store-bought dressing

Supplements: take one capsule of whole food probiotic formula with soil-based organisms, one capsule of an immune system support formula with tonic mushrooms, one capsule of an adaptogenic herbal blend with B vitamins, and one to three teaspoons or three to nine capsules of a high omega-3 cod liver oil complex.

Snacks

Drink eight to twelve ounces of water.

no food (partial-fast day)

Before Bed

Drink eight to twelve ounces of water, or hot or iced green tea with honey.

Exercise: go for a short walk outdoors, weather permitting, or walk on an indoor treadmill.

Supplements: make a drink with one tablespoon of raw organic apple cider vinegar and two teaspoons of raw organic honey dissolved in twelve ounces of warm purified water. Drink with two capsules of a systemic enzyme blend with proteases, bromelain, and papain.

Advanced hygiene: follow the advanced hygiene recommendations from the morning of Day 1.

Emotional health: follow the forgiveness recommendations from the evening of Day 1.

Body therapy: take a warm bath for fifteen minutes with eight drops of biblical essential oils added.

Purpose: ask yourself these questions: "Did I live a life of purpose today?" "What did I do to add value to someone else's life today?" Commit to living a day of purpose tomorrow.

Prayer: thank God for this day, asking Him to give you a restoring night's rest and a fresh start tomorrow. Thank Him for His steadfast love that never ceases and His mercies that are new every morning. Read Isaiah 58:6–9 aloud.

Sleep: go to bed by half past ten.

DAY 6 (REST DAY)

Upon Waking

Prayer: thank God because this is the day that the Lord has made. Rejoice and be glad in it. Thank Him for the breath in your lungs and the life in your body. Read Psalm 23 aloud.

Purpose: ask the Lord to give you an opportunity to add significance to someone's life today. Watch for that opportunity. Ask God to use you this day for His intended purpose.

Advanced hygiene: follow the advanced hygiene recommendations from Day 1.

Reduce toxins: follow the recommendations for reducing toxins from Day 1.

Morning supplements: make a drink with one tablespoon of raw organic apple cider vinegar and two teaspoons of raw organic honey dissolved in twelve ounces of warm purified water. Drink with two capsules of a systemic enzyme blend with proteases, bromelain, and papain.

Exercise: no formal exercise; it's a rest day.

Body therapies: none; it's a rest day.

Emotional health: follow the emotional health recommendations from the morning of Day 1.

Breakfast

Drink one cup of hot or iced green tea with honey.

two or three omega-3 eggs cooked any style in one tablespoon of extra virgin coconut oil

two ounces of smoked wild salmon

one grapefruit or orange

handful of almonds

Supplements: take one capsule of whole food probiotic formula with soil-based organisms, one capsule of an immune system support formula with tonic mushrooms, and one capsule of an adaptogenic herbal blend with B vitamins.

Lunch

Before eating, drink eight ounces of water.

During lunch, drink eight ounces of water, or hot or iced green tea with honey.

large green salad with mixed greens, avocado, carrots, cucumbers, celery, tomatoes, red cabbage, red peppers, red onions, and sprouts, adding two ounces of low mercury, high omega-3 tuna

salad dressing: mix extra virgin olive oil, apple cider vinegar or lemon juice, minced fresh garlic, naturally brewed soy sauce, Celtic sea salt, herbs, and spices together; or, mix one tablespoon of extra virgin olive oil with one tablespoon of a healthy store-bought dressing

one organic apple with the skin

Supplements: take one capsule of whole food probiotic formula with soil-based organisms, one capsule of an immune system support formula with tonic mushrooms, and one capsule of an adaptogenic herbal blend with B vitamins.

Dinner

Before eating, drink eight ounces of water.

During dinner, drink hot or iced green tea with honey.

roasted organic chicken

cooked vegetables (carrots, onions, peas, etc.)

large green salad with mixed greens, avocado, carrots, tomato, red cabbage, red onions, red peppers, and sprouts

salad dressing: mix extra virgin olive oil, apple cider vinegar or lemon juice, minced fresh garlic, naturally brewed soy sauce, Celtic sea salt, herbs, and spices together; or, mix one tablespoon of extra virgin olive oil with one tablespoon of a healthy store-bought dressing

Supplements: take one capsule of whole food probiotic formula with soil-based organisms, one capsule of an immune system support formula with tonic mushrooms, one capsule of an adaptogenic herbal blend with B vitamins, and one-to-three teaspoons or three-to-nine capsules of a high omega-3 cod liver oil complex.

Snacks

Drink eight to twelve ounces of water, or hot or iced green tea with honey.

one piece of organic fruit

one berry antioxidant whole food nutrition bar with beta-glucans from soluble oat fiber

Before Bed

Drink eight to twelve ounces of water, or hot tea with honey.

Exercise: go for a short walk outdoors, weather permitting, or walk on an indoor treadmill.

Supplements: make a drink with one tablespoon of raw organic apple cider vinegar and two teaspoons of raw organic honey dissolved in twelve ounces of warm purified water. Drink with two capsules of a systemic enzyme blend with proteases, bromelain, and papain.

Advanced hygiene: follow the advanced hygiene recommendations from the morning of Day 1.

Emotional health: follow the forgiveness recommendations from the evening of Day 1.

Purpose: ask yourself these questions: "Did I live a life of purpose today?" "What did I do to add value to someone else's life today?" Commit to living a day of purpose tomorrow.

Prayer: thank God for this day, asking Him to give you a restoring night's rest and a fresh start tomorrow. Thank Him for His steadfast love that never ceases and His mercies that are new every morning. Read Psalm 23 aloud.

Body therapy: spend ten minutes listening to soothing music before you retire.

Sleep: go to bed by half past ten.

DAY 7

Upon Waking

Prayer: thank God because this is the day that the Lord has made. Rejoice and be glad in it. Thank Him for the breath in your lungs and the life in your body. Read Psalm 91 aloud.

Purpose: ask the Lord to give you an opportunity to add significance to someone's life today. Watch for that opportunity. Ask God to use you this day for His intended purpose.

Advanced hygiene: follow the advanced hygiene recommendations from Day 1.

Reduce toxins: follow the recommendations for reducing toxins from Day 1.

Morning supplements: make a drink with one tablespoon of raw organic apple cider vinegar and two teaspoons of raw organic honey dissolved in twelve ounces of warm purified water. Drink with two capsules of a systemic enzyme blend with proteases, bromelain, and papain.

Exercise: begin by performing functional fitness exercises for five minutes or spend five minutes on a mini-trampoline. Finish with five minutes of deep-breathing exercises. Caution: the following exercises are designed to be gentle on the body and should be energizing—not draining. If you are suffering from extreme fatigue, please start slowly. (One to three rounds of the exercises can be found at www.BiblicalHealth Institute.com.)

Body therapy: get twenty minutes of direct sunlight sometime during the day, but be careful between ten o'clock in the morning and two o'clock in the afternoon.

Emotional health: follow the emotional health recommendations from the morning of Day 1.

Breakfast

Make a smoothie in a blender with the following ingredients:

1 cup plain yogurt or kefir (sheep's milk is best)

1 tablespoon organic flaxseed oil

1–2 tablespoons raw organic honey

1 cup of organic fruit (berries, banana, peaches, pineapple, etc.)

2 tablespoons goat's milk protein powder

dash of vanilla extract (optional)

Supplements: take one capsule of whole food probiotic formula with soil-based organisms, one capsule of an immune system support formula with tonic mushrooms, and one capsule of an adaptogenic herbal blend with B vitamins.

Lunch

Before eating, drink eight ounces of water.

During lunch, drink eight ounces of water, or hot or iced green tea with honey.

large green salad with mixed greens, avocado, carrots, tomato, red cabbage, red onions, red peppers, and sprouts, adding three ounces of cold, poached, or canned wild-caught salmon

salad dressing: mix extra virgin olive oil, apple cider vinegar or lemon juice, minced fresh garlic, naturally brewed soy sauce, Celtic sea salt, herbs, and spices together; or, mix one tablespoon of extra virgin olive oil with one tablespoon of a healthy store-bought dressing

one piece of fruit in season

Supplements: take one capsule of whole food probiotic formula with soil-based organisms, one capsule of an immune system support formula with tonic mushrooms, and one capsule of an adaptogenic herbal blend with B vitamins.

Dinner

Before eating, drink eight ounces of water.

During dinner, drink hot tea with honey.

baked or grilled fish of your choice

steamed broccoli

baked sweet potato with butter

large green salad with mixed greens, avocado, carrots, tomato, red cabbage, red onions, red peppers, and sprouts

salad dressing: mix extra virgin olive oil, apple cider vinegar or lemon juice, minced fresh garlic, naturally brewed soy sauce, Celtic sea salt, herbs, and spices together; or, mix one tablespoon of extra virgin olive oil with one tablespoon of a healthy store-bought dressing

Supplements: take one capsule of whole food probiotic formula with soil-based organisms, one capsule of an immune system support formula with tonic mushrooms, one capsule of an adaptogenic herbal blend with B vitamins, and one to three teaspoons or three to nine capsules of a high omega-3 cod liver oil complex.

Snacks

Drink eight to twelve ounces of water, or hot or iced green tea with honey.

apple slices with raw sesame butter (tahini)

one berry antioxidant whole food nutrition bar with beta-glucans from soluble oat fiber

Before Bed

Drink eight to twelve ounces of water, or hot or iced green tea with honey.

Exercise: go for a short walk outdoors, weather permitting, or walk on an indoor treadmill.

Supplements: make a drink with one tablespoon of raw organic apple cider vinegar and two teaspoons of raw organic honey dissolved in twelve ounces of warm purified water. Drink with two capsules of a systemic enzyme blend with proteases, bromelain, and papain.

Advanced hygiene: follow the advanced hygiene recommendations from the morning of Day 1.

Emotional health: follow the forgiveness recommendations from the evening of Day 1.

Body therapy: take a warm bath for fifteen minutes with eight drops of biblical essential oils added.

Purpose: ask yourself these questions: "Did I live a life of purpose today?" "What did I do to add value to someone else's life today?" Commit to living a day of purpose tomorrow.

Prayer: thank God for this day, asking Him to give you a restoring night's rest and a fresh start tomorrow. Thank Him for His steadfast love that never ceases and His mercies that are new every morning. Read 1 Corinthians 13:4–8 aloud.

Sleep: go to bed by half past ten.

DAY 8 AND BEYOND

If you're feeling better, you can repeat the Great Physician's Rx for Chronic Fatigue and Fibromyalgia Battle Plan as many times as you'd like. For detailed step-by-step suggestions and meal and lifestyle plans, visit www.GreatPhysiciansRx.com and join the 40-Day Health Experience for continued good health. Or, you may be interested in the Lifetime of Wellness plan if you want to maintain your newfound level of health. These online programs will provide you with customized daily meal and exercise plans and provide you the tools to track your progress.

If you've experienced positive results from the Great Physician's Rx for Chronic Fatigue and Fibromyalgia program, I encourage you to reach out to someone you know and recommend this book and Battle Plan to them. You can learn how to lead a small group at your church or home by visiting www.BiblicalHealthInstitute.com.

Remember: you don't have to be a doctor or a health expert to help transform the life of someone you care about—you just have to be willing.

Allow me to offer this prayer of blessing from Numbers 6:24–26 (NKJV) to you:

> The LORD bless you and keep you;
> The LORD make His face shine upon you,
> And be gracious to you;
> The LORD lift up His countenance upon you,
> And give you peace.

Need Recipes?

For a detailed list of over two hundred healthy and delicious recipes contained in the Great Physician's Rx eating plan, please visit www.BiblicalHealthInstitute.com.

NOTES

Introduction

1. "Chronic Fatigue Syndrome," *Wikipedia*, http://en.wikipedia.org/wiki/Chronic_fatigue_syndrome (accessed February 19, 2007).

2. "NIAMS Funds Multiple Research Grants in Fibromyalgia," National Institutes of Health, http://www.nih.gov/news/pr/jul99/niams-08.htm (accessed July 8, 1999).

3. David Ian Miller, "Finding My Religion: Chronic Fatigue Syndrome Led Jessica Mapes to Her Spiritual Path," *San Francisco Chronicle*, March 28, 2005.

4. "Stress, Childhood Trauma Linked to Chronic Fatigue Syndrome in Adults," EurekaAlert!, http://www.eurekalert.org/pub_releases/2006-11/jaaj-sct110206.php (Accessed June 7, 2007).

5. Trivieri, Larry, ed. *Alternative Medicine: The Definitive Guide* (Berkeley, CA: Celestial Arts, 2002).

6. Claire Williams, "Can the St. John's Wort Herb Help ME/Chronic Fatigue Syndrome Sufferers?" EzineArticles.com, http://ezinearticles.com/?Can-The-St-Johns-Wort-Herb-Help-ME/Chronic-Fatigue-Syndrome-Sufferers?&id-71533 (accessed July 9, 2007).

7. Phyllis A. Balch, C.N.C., *Prescription for Nutritional Healing* (New York: Avery, 2000).

8. Jacob Teitelbaum, M.D., *From Fatigued to Fantastic* (New York: Avery, 2001).

Key #1

1. Trivieri, *Alternative Medicine*).

2. Tom Cowan, M.D., "Ask the Doctor About Chronic Fatigue Syndrome," Weston A. Price Foundation, http://www.westonaprice.org/askdoctor/chronicfatigue.html (accessed February 19, 2007).

3. Rex Russel, *What the Bible Says About Health Living* (Venture, CA: Regal, 1996), 62–63.

4. Sally Fallon and Mary G. Enig, Ph.D., *Nourishing Traditions: The Cookbook that Challenges Politically Correct Nutrition and the Diet Dictocrats* (Washington, DC: NewTrends Publishing, 2000).

5. Paul G. Auwaeter, M.D., ed. "Chicken Soup, Rx for the Cold," Health A to Z, http://www.healthatoz.com/healthatoz/Atoz/dc/caz/resp/cold/chixsoup.jsp (accessed February 19, 2007).

6. Kathleen Fackelmann, "Shake the Salt, Add More Water," *USA Today*, February 12, 2004.

7. Paul Schulick, *Ginger: Common Spice & Wonder Drug*, 3rd ed. (Prescott, AZ: Hohm Press, 1996).

8. F. Batmanghelidj, M.D., *You're Not Sick, You're Thirsty!* (New York: Warner Books, 2003).

Key #2

1. Trivieri, *Alternative Medicine*.

2. James F. Balch, M.D., and Mark Stengler, N.D., *Prescription for Natural Cures* (Ventura, CA: John Wiley & Sons, Inc., 2004).

Key #3

1. Lisa Christopher-Stein, M.D., "Chronic Fatigue Syndrome," MedlinePlus, http://www.nlm.nih.gov/medlineplus/ency/article/001244.htm (accessed February 19, 2007).

2. Jeanie Lerche Davis, "Germs, They're Everywhere," WebMD, http://www.webmd.com/parenting/news/20040623/germs-theyre-everywhere (accessed June 23, 2004).

Key #4

1. Joe Mercola, D.O., "Breakthrough Updates You Need to Know on Vitamin D," http://www.mercola.com/2002/feb/23/vitamin_d.htm (accessed March 19, 2007).

Key #5

1. J. S. Benson and others, *Dental Amalgam: A Scientific Review and Recommended Public Health Strategy for Research, Education, and Regulation*, United States Public Health Service, 1993.

2. ADA Council on Scientific Affairs, "Dental Amalgam: Update on Safety Concerns," *Journal of the American Dental Association* (1998) 129:494-501.

Key #6

1. "Chronic Fatigue Syndrome," Aetna InteliHealth, http://www.intelihealth.com/IH/ihtIH/WSIHW000/9339/9715.html (accessed February 19, 2007).

2. Don Colbert, M.D., *Deadly Emotions* (Nashville, TN: Thomas Nelson Publishers, 2003).

3. Henry Wright, *A More Excellent Way: Be In Health—Spiritual Roots of Disease, Pathways to Wholeness* (Kensington, PA: Anchor, 2003).

About the Authors

Jordan Rubin has dedicated his life to transforming the health of God's people one life at a time. He is the founder and chairman of Garden of Life, Inc., a health and wellness company based in West Palm Beach, Florida, that produces organic functional foods, whole food nutritional supplements, and personal care products and he's a much-in-demand speaker on various health topics.

He and his wife, Nicki, are the parents of a toddler-aged son, Joshua. They make their home in Palm Beach Gardens, Florida.

Joseph D. Brasco, M.D., who has extensive knowledge and experience in gastroenterology and internal medicine, attended medical school at Medical College of Wisconsin in Milwaukee, Wisconsin, and is board certified with the American Board of Internal Medicine. Besides writing for various medical journals, he is also the coauthor of *Restoring Your Digestive Health* with Jordan Rubin. Dr. Brasco is currently in private practice in Huntsville, Alabama.

BHI

BIBLICAL HEALTH
INSTITUTE

The Biblical Health Institute (www.BiblicalHealthInstitute.com) is an online learning community housing educational resources and curricula reinforcing and expanding on Jordan Rubin's Biblical Health message.

Biblical Health Institute provides:

1. "101" level **FREE**, introductory courses corresponding to Jordan's book The Great Physician's Rx for Health and Wellness and its seven keys; Current "101" courses include:

   * "Eating to Live 101"

   * "Whole Food Nutrition Supplements 101"

   * "Advanced Hygiene 101"

   * "Exercise and Body Therapies 101"

   * "Reducing Toxins 101"

   * "Emotional Health 101"

   * "Prayer and Purpose 101"

2. **FREE** resources (healthy recipes, what to E.A.T., resource guide)

3. **FREE** media--videos and video clips of Jordan, music therapy samples, etc.--and much more!

Additionally, Biblical Health Institute also offers in-depth courses for those who want to go deeper.

Course offerings include:

   * 40-hour certificate program to become a Biblical Health Coach

   * A la carte course offerings designed for personal study and growth

   * Home school courses developed by Christian educators, supporting home-schooled students and their parents (designed for middle school and high school ages)

**For more information and updates on these and other resources go to
www.BiblicalHealthInstitute.com**

EXPERIENCE
THE GREAT PHYSICIAN'S Rx
ONLINE

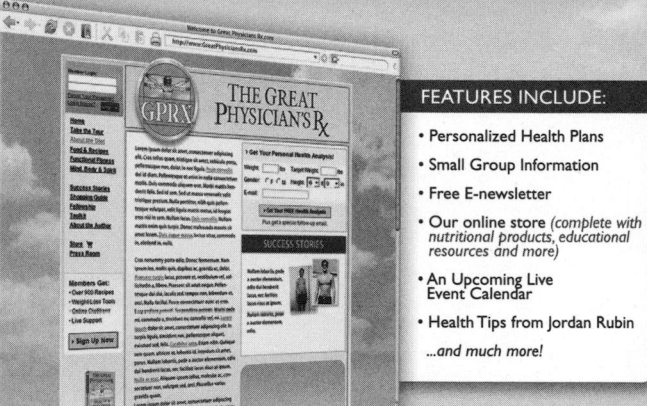

FEATURES INCLUDE:

- Personalized Health Plans
- Small Group Information
- Free E-newsletter
- Our online store *(complete with nutritional products, educational resources and more)*
- An Upcoming Live Event Calendar
- Health Tips from Jordan Rubin

...and much more!

Based on the book *The Great Physician's Rx* by Jordan Rubin, the online experience is your one stop source to **find everything you need to maximize your seven week journey towards abundant health.** Go online today to sign up for our free monthly e-newsletter which includes health tips from Jordan Rubin, specials on products from our online store, and information about live events and small groups in your area.

It's everything you need to unlock your health potential.

WWW.GREATPHYSICIANSRX.COM